AF552832

INFORMATION COMMUNICATION TECHNOLOGY AND ECONOMIC GROWTH

INFORMATION COMMUNICATION TECHNOLOGY AND ECONOMIC GROWTH

By

Dr. M. Lakshmi Narasaiah
M.A., Ph.D.

Professor of Economics
Co-ordinator, Dept. of M.B.A. and Commerce
Special Officer
Sri Krishnadevaraya University Post-graduate Centre
Kurnool–518 002
Andhra Pradesh
(India)

DISCOVERY PUBLISHING HOUSE PVT. LTD.
NEW DELHI-110 002

First Published-2008

ISBN 978-81-8356-306-2

© Author

Published by:

DISCOVERY PUBLISHING HOUSE PVT. LTD.
4831/24, Ansari Road, Prahlad Street,
Darya Ganj, New Delhi-110002 (India)
Phone: 23279245 • Fax: 91-11-23253475
E-mail: dphbooks@rediffmail.com
dphtemp@indiatimes.com
Website: www.discoverypublishinghouse.com

Printed at
Arora Offset Press
Laxmi Nagar, Delhi–92

Preface

The impact of information and communication technology is bringing gradual but often radical change—to working, to learning and more generally to our way of life. Europe has to make the best use of the new technologies. This is particularly crucial in the education and training. Yet schools are often still inadequately equipped with computers and Internet connections. Technology—related skills among the staff concerned, in particularly teachers and trainers, need to be improved. There are significant divergences between countries and regions of this globe. In this situation future is at risk in the increasingly knowledge-driven global economy.

E-Learning

Our definition of 'e-learning' is 'the use of information and communication technology, including the Internet, to learn and teach.

It also designates an initiative to:

- encourage the development and the acquisition of digital literacy;
- improve everyone's capacity to use new technologies for learning and working;
- Adapt our education and training systems to meet the challenges of the information society.

The general objective—to make Europe a major player in the 'new economy'—was agreed in March 2000 by the EU Heads of State of Government in Lisbon, e-learning falls under the European Commission's e-Europe action plan' and 'strategy for employment in the information society. These aim to bring Europe into the digital age.

The objectives:

- to generalize and improve access to hardware, software and to information and communication networks;
- to provide and simplify access to quality training for all of us;
- to develop cooperation between teachers, trainers and managers involved in establishing an educational area;
- to gather and share information on the best practices based on the use of information and communication technology for learning;
- to promote innovation, know-how and expertise.

With Whom

The e-learning initiative is open to cooperation with all interested parties and specialists in education and training, including:

- experts in the used of technologies in the areas of education and training;
- teachers, trainers and project leaders who develop innovative teaching practices in schools, universities and in all other educational establishments;
- senior administrative staff in the education and training sectors;
- pupils trainees, students, all those who want to learn with modern methods;
- information and communication technology companies, multimedia publishers, broadcasters;
- national, regional and local politicians interested in developing e-learning initiatives.

Dr. M. Lakshmi Narasaiah

Contents

1

When Computers Chip Away at Our Memories

Galloping advances in information technology promises to give us instant access to all worlds' knowledge. But how will human memory fare against the rise of the super-machine? If the architects of technology's next great leap forward are to be believed, all knowledge may soon be shrunk to vanishing point. Nanotechnology, or computing carried out at the scale of atoms, is their by word for the future. With its awesome potential, scientists have recently argued, around 11 million 400-page volumes—could be stored and primed for instant viewing on device the size of a human palm.

The ink may still be fresh on these blueprints, but the elixir of portable omniscience no longer seems so far away. Seemingly cast-iron laws of ever increasing computer power, along with the rise of powerful new technologies, appear to point to horizon where all that can be known and remembered can be transferred to machines with which human beings then interact at will. And it is a future that for some is already spelling big trouble for the brain.

Surveys Point to Yawning Gaps in General Knowledge

Computers not only distract us from contemplation of deeper valleys; they discourage from contemplation itself. As surveys repeatedly show, knowledge of history, literature, geography and even current affairs seem to be on a steep decline: 60 per cent of adult Americans cannot recall the name of the president who ordered the dropping of the first atomic bomb, just as 77 per cent of young Britons are perplexed by words Magna Carta. The day of the nano-shrunk library could soon come, but will any of its users be able to remember a single line of poetry?

The connection between these yawning gaps in general knowledge and the information technology is by no means established, but no means established, but a host of thinkers in different fields are sure the issues is one that will shortly become all too pertinent. At the same time as it help us and extends our physically capabilities, it diminishes our individual faculties. This is a vital question, one which has been around for a long time.

Good or evil, writing has nevertheless formed one of the main tools in the evolution of human memory. Indeed it is civilisation's unrelenting hunger for placing memory in external stores—cave paintings then manuscripts, libraries, printed works and finally computers—that has supported the entire march of the species. Each of these new technologies has helped humans "off-load" their memories Pre-literate societies, for instance, depended on oral tradition for their expertise—a practice undermined by the flaws of over worked brains, though fertile ground for epic poetry. Through the written word, memories were freed from the head: knowledge could be stored for retrieval in books, and then redrafted into the sort of novel and complex codes on which modern society is founded.

Becoming Good Memory Managers

The benefits of storing memory outside the brain are unquestionable, but the invention of printing over 500 years ago followed by the post-war onset of computing have added a new note to the process: that of thundering acceleration. One simple equation has come to embody this. It stipulates that computing power—defined in terms of capacity and speed per unit cost-doubles every two years. The trend has held for the last 40 years. Should it continue as expected to around 2020, a personal computer by that year will have exactly the same processing power as a single human brain. Add the promised marvels of nanotechnology, optical and quantum computing, and machines might reach utterly daunting proportions. One penny's worth of computing circa 2099 will have a billion times greater computing capacity than all humans on Earth.

For many cognitive scientists, relations between mind and machine are already undergoing drastic reconfiguration. "Distributed intelligence" is the new maxim, encapsulating all systems in which individuals and computers mesh to carry out a collective task, whether it be landing an aircraft or tracking share prices. The Internet is so far the crowning glory—a system that in principle might combine individual users into a potent group min.

All of this may sound abstract, but the effects on memory are being felt now. Facts and figures no longer take pride of place in school curricula. Within the past two years, South Korea, Singapore and Hong Kong—havens of rote learning—have debated plans to axe huge swathes of standard classroom study. Experts in education stress that students must learn to be adaptable, skilled in manipulating symbols, able to respond to new situations; in short, ready to deal with the new economy, a realm where the computer is king.

We will need a lot of new skills, We have to become good memory managers. We've moved away from managing a lot in our heads to managing memory devices. We have to devote more space to this executive control and less to rote memory storage.

Nurturing Imaginative Thinking at School

A heavy diet of ready-made computer images and programmed toys appears to stunt imaginative thinking. Teachers report that children in our electronic society are becoming alarmingly deficient in generating their own ideas and images. As Generics observes, human memory is much more than simple information processing. There are, for instance, at least five systems of human memory, making up an inordinately rich web of self-reflexive, interweaving recollection that no computer has even come close to imitating. But if memory is increasingly stored in machines that we then manage for our learning, work and leisure, then how will these systems in the brain fare? And how will imagination, intelligence and understanding—all of which depend on an efficiently functioning memory—be affected? The simple answer is: we still do not know.

Yet one image stalks the debate. It is not the old science fiction fear of malevolent computer but of a citizen without a personal memory to speak of, Bertman, for one, is convinced that boundless electronic information may be the deadliest enemy of human knowledge. It's not just enough to remember where we live, what our birthday is, and the name of our wife—there is more to human personality and indentity than just the details we can find inside our wallet.

2

Fleeing the dot.com Era

The Internet has been proclaimed as the supreme network, the place where one day all human beings will communicate. So who are these strange people switching off in droves? Two years ago, one of the scientists behind the original computer language that gave birth to the internet announced a daring new plan. Work would begin, to spread the network beyond the boundaries of earth: the Inter Plan Net, as it has been baptised, would bring online computing to outer space.

Outlandish as it may at first seem, the plan is consistent with the hype and breezy forecasting all too often surrounding discussion of the internet. Even though mounting evidence points to a stubborn "digital divide" separating not just poor and rich countries but also groups within nations, policy-makers, business and computer scientists downplay the figures as brief blips in the unstoppable onward advance of the network.

A figure of a hundred computers per human is not entirely unreasonable, leading to a thousand billion computers in the internet in 2020. This technological optimism has come under increasing scrutiny over the past year. The "Digital Divide," a UN Development Programme report revealed that less than 15 per cent of the world's population accounted for more than 88 per cent of the internet's users. The financial failure of multiple dot.com firms and a sense that the technology is still too slow and unreliable have dented some grander hopes for an "information superhighway." Yet it is a little known and barely noticed trend that may perhaps prove the most troubling: for the first time, evidence has emerged of a widespread tendency to abandon the internet.

No forecasting has yet taken account of this. A cast-iron premise in all extrapolations of the internet's future is that once the network is available, prolonged use necessarily follows.

Recent empirical work has suggested otherwise. Cyber dialogue, an internet research consultancy based in the U.S., has uncovered evidence of a slowdown in internet growth based in interviews with 1,000 users and 1,000 non-users. They argue that the rate of growth is decelerating overall, and that an absolute decline in the number of users aged 18 to 29 is underway. An interesting claim is that approximately one third of U.S. adults simply do not believe they need the internet and what it offers.

The First Signs of a Rebellion Against Commercialisation?

Similarly, a 2000 survey in the U.K. found that 40 per cent of the adult population had no intention of going online, while most of them put their reluctance down either to cost or to the belief that the internet was irrelevant of their lives. Only a third of those who had stopped using the internet expected to reconnect in the future. Cyber dialogue estimated there were 9.4 million former users in the U.S., a figure that had jumped to 27.7 million.

People who stop using the internet, are poorer and less well-educated. Those who are introduced to it via family and friends are more likely to drop out than those who are self-taught or receive formal training. Most surprisingly, teenagers are more likely to give up than people over 20.

These results must be treated with considerable caution, since former users can easily become active ones at a later date. But the sheer existence of internet malcontents—and in such numbers is cyber dialogue is to believed—raises critical challenges to the entire online industry. Why the decision to abandon use just at the time of giant internet expansion prompted by the introduction of the world wide web

Possibly the most salient feature in the trend is how it has coincided with a revolution in the network's character. Though there is as yet no concrete evidence of a link between the two, the suspicion is that the internet's first users have been alienated by the rampant commercialisation of the network over the past five years. Perhaps these figures point to the signs of rebellion against the transformation of a computer-linked community into a marketplace.

During its first 20 years, the network was the preserve of computer science professionals, students and academics resourceful enough to negotiate its complicated protocols. But in 1991, the U.S. national science foundation decided to allow commercial traffic, heralding the internet's switch from academic forum to virtual bazaar. The foundation's decision was followed by the creation of the commercial internet exchange, designed to regulate the exchange of traffic between newly emerging and profit-oriented internet service providers(ISPs).

From four computers connected in 1969, the number grew to 188 by 1979, 159,000 by 1989, and over 56 million world wide by mid 1999. But the decisions of the early 1990s and the emergence of the web-allowing user-friendly multimedia features and full integration of the internet's previously dispersed elements (e-mail, file transfer and information access)—also marked a change in style. The temptations of advertising on and profiting from this unique interface soon proved overwhelming. The proportion of internet computer addresses ending with .com or .net, and thus in the private sector, has risen steeply as a result. By 1999, these addresses formed 79 per cent of the internet, up from 47 per cent four years earlier. Over the same period, the public sector share, represented by addresses ending with

.edu, .mil, .gov and .int, fell from 48 to 17 per cent. Non-profit organisations also dropped in their share, from five to two per cent. From their very low base at the end of the 1980s, business shot to a position of dominance within a decade.

There is no doubting that the internet remains an incredibly diverse collection of resources. Much of the original public sector ethos has also remained: most sites are free, and a slew of databases of archives held by companies (particularly the press) are open to whoever wishes to access them.

But it does seem highly probable, if as yet empirically unproven, that the internet's mutation has driven away its first zealots. Back in the 1980s, there was relatively little distinction between the producers of what was on offer on the network and the consumers. If you had the skills and resources needed to access the internet, it was more than likely that you would be able to produce content and even services for it. The ethos was "give some, take some."

A String of Mergers in the Scramble for Supremacy

In the first few years of the web, this interactive culture continued, allowing anyone with a small amount of technical knowledge to become an "internet publisher." The change since then has been profound. Increased emphasis on scripting languages, multimedia and links from the web to databases held by organisations has handed power to skilled, professional programmers now, the medium that was initially conceived and an opportunity for smaller organisations and individuals to create and prosper on a "level playing field" has bifurcated into an industry of producers and a mass of consumers.

This trend was reinforced by the spread of search engines such as yahoo! and Alta Vista, both of which aimed to help the user navigate through the surfeit of internet resources. Commercial extension of this concept has given rise to the "portal"—one of most important elements in the current web industry. While offering traditional search features, these portals also try to maximize revenue by "click-through" advertising and deals with electronic commerce firms. The result of the scramble for portal supremacy has been a string of mergers and takeovers aimed at securing top spot in internet rankings, with leading contenders like AOL, yahoo! and Microsoft acquiring other firms, boosting content, and linking up to media companies such a Disney and ABC network. Ad the era of digital television dawns, this convergence of access and content is certain to accelerate.

There are definitely many users who would not object. Even in its mid-1990s incarnation, use of the internet was plagued by problems of connection, slow movement of data, excesses of information and the off loading of "junk mail." It seems likely that some of those who abandoned the internet did so out of disappointment with the sluggish and haphazard service they received once they had signed up for the promised information revolution.

Such former users could well be tempted back by the latest internet developments. A stress on "pushing" predefined content through portals, sophisticated encryption schemes, secure payment systems and faster connections all promise to make the network easier to use and navigate, while simultaneously reducing variety. Add to this the fragmentation of the internet through its introduction in mobile phone, interactive television and palmtops, and it is clear that the marriage between access and content—between the device that leads the user into the network and what the user sees—may well become much tighter. The result could be absolute commercialisation.

The Symbolic Value of Joining the Information Highway

This goes to show that the requirements of different groups of users, and particularly groups of former users, are not necessarily the same. The more commercial the network becomes, the more it strays from its free and interactive origins, the more likely certain users will be turned of. A different group of users, on the other hand, might switch off were it to remain chaotic and technical.

Certain trends may help to bridge this gap. The number and breadth of internet resources is still growing, as is the quantity of local content made outside the United States. Simple text message services sent via low-speed telecoms—the so-called "information dirt track"—could also speed the take-up of the internet throughout the developing world, evading the costly trap of commercial, high-speed service providers.

But a whole set of premises about the exponential increase in use of the internet and the loyalty of internet users are under threat. At present, the symbolic value of having internet access is mainly perceived as a sigh of inclusion in an unspecified, high-technology future. Its rejection can be seen to imply a refusal of the intimidating, exhausting pace of technological and social innovation. The internet may travel to space, but it still has convincing to do on earth.

3

e-Learning—Designing Tomorrow's Education

The impact of information and communication technology is bringing gradual but often radical change—to working, to learning and more generally to our way of life. Europe has to make the best use of the new technologies. This is particularly crucial in the education and training. Yet schools are often still inadequately equipped with computers and Internet connections. Technology-related skills among the staff concerned, in particularly teachers and trainers, need to be improved. There are significant divergences between countries and regions of this globe. In this situation future is at risk in the increasingly knowledge-driven global economy.

e-Learning

Our definition of 'e-learning' is 'the use of information and communication technology, including the internet, to learn and teach.

It also designates an initiative to:

- encourage the development and the acquisition of digital literacy;
- improve everyone's capacity to use new technologies for learning and working;
- Adapt our education and training systems to meet the challenges of the information society.

The general objective—to make Europe a major player in the 'new economy'—was agreed in March 2000 by the EU Heads of State of Government in Lisbon, e-learning falls under the European Commission's 'e-Europe Action Plan' and 'Strategy for Employment in the Information Society'. These aim to bring Europe into the digital age.

The objectives:

- to generalize and improve access to hardware, software and to information and communication networks;
- to provide and simplify access to quality training for all of us;
- to develop cooperation between teachers, trainers and managers involved in establishing an educational area;
- to gather and share information on the best practices based on the use of information and communication technology for learning;
- to promote innovation, know-how and expertise.

With Whom

The e-learning initiative is open to cooperation with all interested parties and specialists in education and training, including:

- experts in the used ᵒf technologies in the areas of education and training;
- teachers, trainers and project leaders who develop innovative teaching practices in schools, universities and in all other educational establishments;
- senior administrative staff in the education and training sectors;
- pupils trainees, students, all those who want to learn with modern methods;

- **information and communication technology companies, multimedia publishers, broadcasters;**
- **national, regional and local politicians interested in developing e-learning initiatives.**

4

The dot.bomb Syndrome

Every one agrees that privacy is good for business. But is there a market for companies offering to protect it? While several firms have recently suffered class-action lawsuits and public outrage over apparent intrusions into customers personal data, American Express is one of a number of businesses that may be blazing the right path from privacy to profits.

Last year, the credit card issuer rolled out "Private Payments", enabling its customers to go online and obtain "Disposable" credit card numbers that could be used for only one online purchase. If the number was ever stolen after being used for purchase, it would be worthless.

A key lesson is that protecting privacy, in this case the credit card number, became an "enhanced value" to an existing service. Moreover, American Express understood that the credit card number was the "tip of the privacy iceberg"—it plans to roll out a suite of related services, like anonymous Internet browsing, in 2001. Rival companies like Visa/ Mastercard, are following the same trail.

Another company to watch is PrivaSys, of San Francisco, which has patented technology to enable plastic credit cards to generate disposal numbers for each purchase privaSys does this by equipping the card with a calculator-styled key pad and LCD screen, a very thin battery, and a special magnetic stripe. The card holder punches a 4-digit PIN into the credit card itself and—Voila!—the card generates the disposable number.

But securing payments is just one part of an emerging privacy protection market. Other firms are offering anonymous or "Pseudonymous" browsing tools, packages to control cookies—the strings of code that are planted on the user's computer by websites—and services to block hacker intrusion. Only time will tell which companies will control niche markets or achieve critical mass.

What's, clear is that the nascent e-commerce industry badly miscalculated the importance of privacy to their business model. For without privacy, there was no consumer confidence, and without such confidence, e-commerce, had no chance of fulfilling the short-term, high expectations that initially sent their stock values soaring. The current shake-out of the "dot.bomb" industry shows how costly this miscalculation over privacy was.

An Added But Essential Value

But if you thought privacy was a big issue for e-commerce, consider the debate on the wireless industry. Referred to as Mobile or M-commerce, this industry appears to have unlimited potential to deliver information and location-based services, advertisements, and discounts coupons to cellular phones and hand-held wireless devices. M-commerce risks hitting the major "Privacy buttons": constant surveillance via location-based tracking; unsolicited ads clogging communication devices; detailed profiles of individuals interest and movements; and insecure payment mechanisms.

Nonetheless, the industry is showing signs that it has learned from the mistakes of e-commerce. A few months ago a workshop of the U.S. Federal Trade Commission, leading wireless industry groups unveiled guidelines requiring companies to obtain a consumer's consent before collecting or using personal data. This wasn't altruism: the industry understands that consumers will not tolerate commercial services to their cell phones unless they explicitly consent.

So far, privacy's brief tenure in the commercial market place indicates that some people are willing to pay extra to protect their privacy. But the more important lesson is that consumers are unlikely to take more than a few extra steps to secure their data. If they perceive that a given medium, like the internet is not privacy-friendly, they either change their habitual uses or actually refrain from them altogether. The likelihood is that privacy will become an "added value," creating a market for those who can integrate privacy into payment mechanisms without excessively burdening the consumer.

5

Labour Pains
The Birth of a Movement

Cyber-rights and business groups are fighting a proposed cybercrime treaty. While there is strength in numbers, the groups' diversity may prove too much for the coalition to bear. An eclectic coalition of civil rights and corporate groups however, has launched an offensive against the proposed cybercrime treaty as well as a battery of controversial national laws and international standards.

Not surprisingly, the first privacy campaign emerged in the U.S. an internet stronghold, against the infamous Clipper Chip. According to the government, this cryptographic device would have offered a standard for securing private voice communication. Two government agencies would have held the "keys", to be handed out only with "legal authorisation". Privacy-minded citizens quickly saw the dangers of this in light of the federal government's history of illegal domestic surveillance. In 1994, 50,000 people—a hefty chunk of the cybernaut population—signed the largest internet petition of its time against the proposal, which died soon after.

Perhaps the most striking feature in the battle to protect privacy has been the diversity of groups involved. The year 1996 saw a motley crew of immigration groups, gun-owners, liberals and conservatives band together to oppose legislation that would notably have extended wiretapping and allowed for more investigations of political groups. Irish-American and Arab-American associations joined out of concern that they would be more aggressively targeted in the "war on terrorism". Meanwhile, the fear of a more invasive government rallied gun-owners alongside groups from across the ideological spectrum. Once again, by tapping the Internet's power to organize and disseminate information, they shelved the legislation.

But this ad hoc co-operation is based on shaky ground. There was considerable coordination, for example, between civil liberties groups and the industry to oppose the 1994 Communications Assistance for Law Enforcement Act, which requires telecommunications carriers to modify their equipment, facilities and services in order to comply with authorised electronic surveillance. Yet once the industry received a promise of government funding to implement the law, it quickly abandoned the coalition. Corporate representatives then jumped sides again and sued the government over implementation rules in a controversy that is still brewing.

Old Enemies Become New Allies

With the internet's growth, the privacy battle is becoming increasingly international. Most Western European countries have at least one cyber-rights group, a trend that is spreading across the continent and Asia, particularly in Japan. At the same time, existing human rights groups have also started to focus on the internet. All it takes is for a single national government to ban free speech on the Web and the issue instantly takes on a global character.

For decades, international bodies like the Organisation for Economic Co-operation and Development (OECD), the Council of Europe and the European Union (EU) have been developing international standards relating to privacy, free speech and other civil liberties issues. Their work has included brokering common rules on data protection and encryption policy to promote e-commerce. While some government representatives have put a stronger emphasis on protecting human rights, economic interests have clearly dominated the debate, strongly influenced by the International Chamber of Commerce, a powerful lobby of industry groups. Today, by pressuring governments bilaterally and multilaterally, the U.S. is leading the efforts to expand surveillance worldwide. This pressure amounts to what privacy advocates call "policy laundering": by pushing other governments into accepting controversial plans like the Clipper Chip, international standards will be developed which will in turn force the U.S. Congress to accept proposals it had originally rejected.

To respond with more muscle to these trends, a new opposition front emerged in 1996—the Global Internet Liberty Campaign (GILC), started by the Electronic Privacy Information Center, Human Rights Watch and the American Civil Liberties Association. The group now represents over 50 NGOs from some 30 countries. GLIC operates by consensus. Member organisations propose specific actions such as drafting letters to world leaders, releasing reports and holding conferences. Member groups then agree to join in the action.

GLIC and groups like the Trans-Atlantic Consumer Dialogue (TACD) are making inroads into the policy processes. Perhaps the most tangible signs of their success are the frequent invitations to participate in OECD meetings. But the movement has just one foot in the door: the next step lies in strengthening the role of NGOs outside the U.S. The problem lies in the old Achilles heel of international movements—a lack of funding.

6

Wiring up the Ivory Towers

Prestigious universities are forging alliances to conquer a share of the e-learning market and stand up to virtual competitors. Just like airline companies, universities around the world are forming partnerships and consortia in response to the pressures of globalisation. The World Education Market held in Vancouver was a timely sign: the fair, expressly organised to foster relations between universities, training providers, software companies and representatives from nations with large education needs attracted participants from over 60 countries.

This race to "partner up" is fuelled by a number of factors. In most industrialised countries, government funding for higher education has decreased, forcing institutions to look for new markets either to subsidize campus programmes or just to remain viable. There is a growing need for lifelong learning as "jobs for life" vanish and the information society drastically reduces the shelf-life of almost any educational qualification. Technological developments, increasingly necessary for learners in all fields to master, offer ever more innovative tools for supporting e-learning.

For business, online learning is "the" new market opportunity with the need for re-training and professional updating predicted to increase a $11.5 billion industry by 2003. Business is better able to develop and maintain the technological infrastructure necessary to run large online systems and everyone, including the universities, recognizes that it takes robust telecommunications technology to deliver education and training on the scale demanded.

A host of companies has sprung up to help universities shape and package courses for online presentation, while network providers are jockeying for position to deliver online education.

The United States is the undisputed leader in the field, prompting governments in the U.K., Canada and Australia to commission being eroded by U.S. ventures turned global Canada and the U.K. are in the early stages of setting up their own virtual universities. But what has become clear is that the conservative and labyrinthine decision-making processes which characterize most university procedures are being jolted by a race to get a share of the lifelong learning market.

So far, the most common approach for universities to break into the e-learning universe has been to develop courses specifically for a corporate partner or to form alliances among themselves. Universitas 21, a company incorporated in the U.K. is a network of 18 leading universities in ten countries.

Very often, prestigious universities has stayed clear of going fully online, seeing a danger to their brand name. Many are limiting their offerings to continuing education programmes and/or non-degree courses, and more often than not, they are aiming at the corporate market. One Company UNext.com, has partnered with first-class institutions such as the University of Columbia (U.S.) and the London School of Economics to create online courses marketed under the name Cardean University. Their target: the Fortune 500 companies as well as individual adults. They've managed to attract nobel laureates to design courses and the universities have formed spin-off for-profit companies specifically to develop online programmes. This facilities the commercialisation of software and other products, and is a way to take a commercial approach to continuing and professional studies without compromising the Univesity's standing.

Then there are the free-standing for profit virtual universities which are arousing the ire of institutions that have prided themselves on a long history of public service. The most quoted examplar is Phoenix University, the largest private outfit in the U.S. Now owned by the Apollo Group, it operates the country's largest online programme with 12,200 students. The university tracks students progress and contacts those who don't submit assignments on time or fail to enrol in subsequent courses. Many critics question Phoenix's blatant commercialisation, but few doubt the university's impact on continuing professional development provision.

Although e-learning is in its infancy, its impact can already by gauged. New providers are coming on the market all the time and the trend is accelerating to the point of upsetting universities virtual monopoly in educational accreditation. An Information Technology training course offered or accredited by Microsoft has undoubtedly become more valuable than a Bachelor of Science from a renowned university.

The more consumerist the approach of the education provider, the more what is taught is influenced by demand. MBAs dominate e-learning provision and IT courses are a close second. While the new consumer/learner demands flexibility, choice and just-in-time learning opportunities, suppliers will inevitably arise who are focused on meeting the demand at the expense of quality and value. And is the consumer really the best judge of what course material to choose? Education is a more complex "product" than toothpaste or washing powder. A totally consumer driven education market is unlikely to be in society's best interest in the long term. The commercialisation of education usually goes hand-in-hand with desegregation: course design, delivery, tutoring assessment and accreditation may be carried out by different organisations. Students might study courses or modules from different universities or providers and then put themselves forward for examination and accreditation by yet another institution. While most academics loathe marking assignments, they regard this scenario with horror, and blame commercialisation for the demise of the 'community of scholars' concept of a university. The death of the 'course' has also been predicted, with learners—especially corporate and on-the job learners—demanding short study modules. What then happens to the ability to get an overview of a field when learning consists of the students selecting a whole series of unconnected learning "bites"? Learners will be "zapping" between short sequences or presentations much as they do between television channels.

But while some faculty view e-learning with alarm, technology-based learning is where most of the pedagogical innovation is taking place in universities. Multimedia learning resources and interactive simulations are being developed for the web. Collaborative learning activities, new forms of online assessment and small group teaching technologies are making online courses more stimulating, interactive and attractive then many face-to-face taught courses.

Despite "doom and gloom scenarios", most moderate observers of the scene see a continued future for the campus university, especially at the undergraduate level, while e-learning will above all cater to adult professional and independent learners. Some commercialisation of education is good if it fosters innovation, concern for quality and responsiveness to consumer demands. But if some is good, more is not necessarily better! Not in education at least.

7

Shaking the Ivory Tower

Universities have changed radically to keep pace with modern life. Now where are they heading in this high-speed age? In the past half century higher education has been transformed from a privilege conferred on social and political elites to a mass activity available to whole populations. This process began in the United States in the 1940s and 1950s, spread to most of Western Europe and many other developed countries during the 1960s and 1970s and in the past two decades has become a global phenomenon. In the next half century it will accelerate, leading perhaps to the replacement of "higher education" (still an elite-ish category despite its expansion) by extended systems of "lifelong learning".

The key to this transformation has been the expansion of secondary education. For example, in all but two countries of the OECD (Organisation for Economic Cooperation and Development) at least two thirds of young people now complete upper secondary education, and so are eligible to enter higher education. The result has been a dramatic increase in enrollment rates in higher education. In Chile the total number of students has grown from 131,000 in 1978 to 235,000 in 1988 and to 343,000 in the mid 1990s. Even in the United States, the pioneer of mass-access higher education where very high secondary education completion rates had already been achieved before 1970, the student population has continued to grow, from 11 million in 1978 to 13 million in 1988 and now to more than 14 million.

Two forces have driven up completion rates in upper secondary education and enrollment rates in higher education. The first has been democratisation. As late as 1945 high levels of social, and hence educational, inequality persisted even in democratic countries, and much of the world remained in the grip of colonial and totalitarian powers. In North America, Western Europe and Australasia democratisation typically took the form of the development of "welfare states" in which there was an increase in public expenditure on education, housing, health and social security that was sustained over more than three decades after the end of the Second World War.

More recently, as renewed emphasis has been placed on the market even in social policy, the rise of consumerism has continued to fuel demands for increased higher education opportunities. The older idea of education as a civil entitlement has been compounded by newer notions of free access to the education marketplace. Far from arresting the advance to mass higher education, consumerism has accelerated it in most developed countries. As traditional forms of social differentiation based on class, gender and ethnic origin have been eroded by democratisation and by market forces, new forms based on educational certification have become more important. In many developed countries the middle class and the "graduate class" have tended to coalesce.

In much of Asia and Africa democratisation took the form of decolonisation. In newly independent countries the energy originally generated in liberation struggles against the colonial powers was directed into a wider struggle to create fairer and more equal successor societies. Education was central to this struggle. The result has been a rapid increase in higher education enrollment, for example, in Tunisia from barely 2,000 students at the time of independence to more than 100,000 today. That process continues.

However, the relationship between democratisation and the development of higher education has been less straightforward in developing countries. Despite very rapid rates of expansion the "metropolitan" influences of the former colonial powers have lingered more stubbornly in higher education than at other levels of education. This is partly due to the continued influence of associations between universities in the British Commonwealth as well as those between francophone universities.

Partly because of these lingering "metropolitan" models and partly because levels of participation are still lower than in developed countries, many African or Asian universities have remained more elite institutions than higher education institutions in North America and Europe. Also, as economic conditions have worsened in some developing countries, the competition between primary and higher education sharpened in the post-independence years as both were seen as equally important priorities. This competition was often reinforced by the intervention of the World Bank.

The second force driving up higher education enrollments has been the changing nature of the labour market. Traditional occupations have become comparatively less significant, while new service occupations, which often require graduate-level skills, have become more important.

Skill requirements have been become more sophisticated. Jobs once done by unskilled or semi-skilled workers are now undertaken by technicians; and those which as recently as the 1980s were taken by technicians are now likely to be filled by graduates. The capital invested for every worker has more than doubled in the past 20 years. Even in occupations where there is less evidence that skills contents have changed significantly, university graduates are now employed in much larger numbers, partly to enhance the social status of these occupations and partly to compete in a graduate-dominated labour market. Healthcare is a good example. Once doctors were the only graduates; today, many para-medical workers are also trained in higher education.

The second form taken by the economic driver has been the growing conviction that national success now depends on economic competitiveness which, in the context of a knowledge-based economy, depends in turn on an adequate supply of human capital. Knowledge is now seen as the key economic resource.

This analysis my be exaggerated; raw materials are still very important in national economies and the global economy. But it has become pervasive and persuasive. The naïve and linear theories of human capital popular a generation ago which postulated a direct link between investment in education and economic growth may have been challenged; some forms of higher education are now as likely to be labelled consumption as investment goods. Nevertheless, the discourse of the "Knowledge Society" has become even more powerful.

The impact of democratisation and economic competitiveness on higher education has been immense. First, the expansion of student numbers has made the cost of higher education a significant element within national budgets for the first time. A number of important consequences has flowed from this—the opportunity, and incentive, to compare the value of investing in different levels of education; increasing demands that universities are run as efficiently as possible (compromising their traditional autonomy from the state—and the market); lower unit costs as budgets have been trimmed (which may have undermined higher education's claim to represent academic excellence). Second, higher education systems have emerged that embrace not only traditional universities but also non-university institutions. Two effects have been produced. One is that the ethos of the traditional university has been eroded; it no longer stands in glorious isolation. The other is that institutional differentiation has been encouraged, whether through active state planning or in response to markets for teaching and research.

The prospects for the next half century are for an acceleration of both drivers—to include access to higher education among the basic entitlements enjoyed by citizens in democratic societies; and to "put knowledge to work" in order to generate wealth and to improve the quality of life. The prospects for higher education during the same period are also relatively easy to predict increased efficiency (which is likely to include growing pressure to make students contribute more to the cost of their higher education); greater accountability, although more probably in a "market" than a "planning" mode as even the state redefines its role as the purchaser of higher education services, more differentiation, both between and within higher education institutions, as they struggle to identify markets niches; and possibly growing demands that higher education become more relevant as instrumental considerations triumph over idealistic ones.

However, the future may be more complex than the past. In the second half of the 20th century the encounter between higher education and society has been comparatively straightforward. Although dynamic, society has presented a familiar enough face. It was characterised by a combination of bureaucratic rationality and secular (and liberal) individualism. The beneficence of science and technology was uncontested. The dominant economic model was of large scale industry, or analogous organisations in the corporate and public sectors. Although rapidly evolving, concepts and categories like "career" and "profession" remained valid. Higher education too was familiar enough. Despite the great expansion of student numbers and its adoption of novel roles, the university continued to be recognizable as such. Other types of higher education institution have been deeply influenced by university values and practices.

In the first half of the 21st century both society and higher education may become problematical and so contested categories. Some of these uncertainties are already emerging. Once firm demarcations between public and private domains, whether in terms of the balance between the state and the market or between social "spaces" and individual desires; between producers and users; between investment and consumption; between work and leisure are becoming increasingly fuzzsy in the emerging post-industrial society. Wealth is being generated by the production of "symbolic" as well as—or more than—material goods. Value is created by design, sales, marketing, service rather than by primary production. Institutions of all kinds, civic and corporate, are being challenged by the rise of adaptable and flexible organisations, made possible by advances in communications and information technology.

The force of globalisation amounts to much more than round-the clock—round-the world financial markets or an emerging international division of labour; it is not only undermining nation states but also reconfiguring time and space to produce global intimacies, again with the help of the information revolution. Social identities are no longer moulded by the "givens" of religion, class and gender, or by positions within the occupational structure, as they have been since the advent of the industrial revolution in Europe two centuries ago. Instead they are being subsumed by a process of individualisation in which life-styles rather than life-chances predominate.

Higher education will have not only to continue to satisfy the predictable demands for democratic entitlement and socio-economic utility with which it is familiar, but also to cope with the consequences of these new uncertainties. These may include; new curricula that emphasis style and images at the expense of skills and information; recategorisation of higher education as a playful, even selfish, activity; a tighter link between experience of higher education and social esteem; submergence of the universal, but also particular, values characteristic of the traditional university by anomic globalisation; threats to the scientific tradition and methods, from the "risk society", from subjectivisation and from demands that other knowledge traditions are accorded equal respect.

The universities of the 21st century, therefore, may have to face two ways. They will have to continue to pay attention to the democratisation and the "knowledge society" agendas, which are likely both to be subsumed in a larger "lifelong learning" agenda. Their ability to sustain current levels of public funding and to satisfy their student-customers will depend on their success in this respect. It will not be easy. There is a danger that the essence of higher education will be lost if it succumbs to unconstrained populism. If this happens, the "quality" of the university will disappear—and with it perhaps its distinctiveness and so its utility and marketability. Similarly in the knowledge Society of the future the university will face new rivals because all organisations will need to become "learning organisations". These rivals strength will be increased if the superiority of universal science is successfully challenged.

But universities will also have to address the new agendas—or the "death" of work (land graduate careers?), of new social movements (and the erosion of individual enlightenment, of globalisation and virtualisation (and the undermining of academic community?); of "alternative" knowledge traditions and, perhaps even, anti-cognitive values with the undermining of "objective" science and further erosion of a common intellectual culture.

8

Shhh... They're Listening

The journalist who first uncovered Echelon, a major electronic spy network, reveals how international surveillance touches us all. Constellations of giant golf balls can be spotted in the most remote locations across the world, from China's Pamir mountains to the swampy north coast of Australia and atop tiny coral atolls in the Indian Ocean. Between 30 and 50 metres wide, these smooth, symmetrical white domes also loom among rice fields in northern Japan and the vineyards and mountains of New Zealand's Island.

The clusters are the most visible signs of concealed electronic network that watch the world. Each dome is filled with satellite tracking dishes that silently soak up and examine millions of taxes, e-mail messages, phone calls and computer data that keep business and political affairs afloat. Unknown to the communicators, their messages are running through the domes, into computer networks and onto listeners who may be on the other side of the planet.

As the world has globalised and international communications have become central to human affairs, these listening networks have grown exponentially. They are part of systems called signals intelligence or "sigint", operated by a handful of advanced countries.

For many years, sigint networks were secret: discussion of their existence was strongly discouraged or even forbidden by law in the countries concerned. Now the European Parliament is seriously investigating sigint organisations and their impact on human rights and international trade. Europe is focusing on "Echelon", a system that relies on listening stations in about ten countries to intercept and process international satellite communications. Echelon is just one part of an immense network run by the U.S. and its English-speaking allies—Britain, Canada, Australia and New Zealand—known as UKUSA after a secret agreement that created the alliance in 1948. Little escapes the UKUSA network, which intercepts messages from the internet, undersea cables and radio transmissions as well as from monitoring equipment installed in embassies. It even operates in space with a fleet of orbiting satellites.

The history of systems like Echelon is as old as radio itself. The first international scandal over secret listening occurred in the 1920s, when the U.S. Senate discovered that British agents were copying every international telegram sent by American telegraph companies. Today's international networks were founded in the early years of the Cold War, when many western countries began jointly monitoring the former Soviet Union.

Fear Not the Word "Bomb"

Who is listened to, and why? Officially governments only admit that surveillance is aimed at commonly agreed perils such as arms proliferation, terrorism, drug trafficking and the organised crime. But this is the tip of the iceberg. The main aim is to spy on other governments' diplomatic messages and military plans while collecting information about trade. In fact, in 1992, the U.S. re-adjusted its national intelligence priorities, specifying that 40 per cent would be economic or "economic in nature".

While UKUSA is the world's largest network, France, Germany and the Russian Federation have similar systems. On a smaller scale, so do countries in Scandinavia and the Middle East, including Israel, Saudi Arabia and the Gulf states. The budges of all government sigint agencies probably add up to an annual expenditure of $20 billion, according to my calculations for a European Parliament report published last year.

Despite the extraordinary scale of Echelon and its sister systems, the press has mistakenly reported that the network could intercept "all e-mail, telephone, and fax communications". Nor can it recognize the content of every telephone call. And it is pure fiction that by typing key words like "bomb" in an e-mail, you can trigger a tape recorder in some secret base. For every million messages or phone calls intercepted, less than 10 will be used for intelligence purposes. Most personal communications are ignored except those of "important" individuals, like politicians, top business executives and their families.

The UKUSA network, however, does have the power to access and process most of the world's satellite communications and relay contents to client states. The system provides participating countries an enormous, unfair political advantage, since most developing nations cannot afford the expertise and equipment necessary to protect the privacy and security of their works.

Spying on the Government for the People

News about these systems began to leak out in the 1970s as U.S. intelligence agencies came under scrutiny in the "Watergate" affair, when former president Richard Nixon used electronic bugging against his election opponents. Since then, an increasing number of whistleblowers have revealed the scale and effects of sign spying.

Over the next 20 years, official secrecy relaxed as U.S. Congressional investigations notably turned the spotlight on sigint agencies. In Britain in the 1980s, a controversial ban on trade union membership at the Government Communications Headquarters (GCHQ) boomeranged by shifting attention on its spying activities.

The growth of the public information culture on the internet has taken these developments a step further. Now, even GCHQ and NSA have websites to reassure UKUSA citizens that they are not targets. No such safeguards apply to the rest of the world: these citizens are by default denied the right to privacy. The countries intercepting their communications are free to use the intelligence for whatever they wish.

Such conduct violates the Universal Declaration of Human Rights, and the International Telecommunications Convention, which assures the privacy of international communications. Indeed sigint agencies trample over a long line of treaties.

While individuals probably never know that they have been spied upon, their organisations and countries may pay a high price for it. During trade negotiations, sigint agencies can sweep up the messages of a producer nation to discover their bottom line. Armed with such secret reports, the negotiators for the developed world can force prices down to a minimum. Several governments have recently begun targeting environmental organisations or those protesting unfair world trade.

Even when there are no direct adverse consequences, the mere existence of powerful surveillance systems can exercise a chilling effect on free speech, inhibiting political and cultural development.

As these activities have become more controversial, the U.S. has tried to expand its circle of collaborators. Countries like Switzerland and Denmark are currently building new satellite stations to gather and trade spy data with the U.S. But, as the ongoing European Parliament inquiry indicates, public awareness and concern are growing fast. Yet vigilance is not enough: if countries and peoples are to have equal rights in the global information infrastructure, concerted action must quickly follow.

9

Globalisation and Knowledge Divide

Globalisation looks very different when it is seen, not from the capitals of the West, but from the cities and villages of the South, where most of humanity lives. Four examples taken from India, illustrate how the paradoxical forces shaping globalisation look when seen from the other side.

Five school children died in a remote village in India after drinking water and powdered milk mixed in a vat that had contained a powerful insecticide. Nobody could read the label of the vat and the children were poisoned. The insecticide in question has been banned in practically every industrialised nation; its sale continues only in places like my country.

Secondly, an important annual event recently took place in North India. Potato growers gather there to exchange the best seeds they have produced in the last year. It is an act of pride for communities to share with others seeds that will help improve the production of potatoes. A transnational corporation attended the festival and are now working to patent the genes of these traditional foodstuffs in order to sell them as profit.

India's macro-economic indicators are excellent. In the offices of investment bankers, you will be told that India is a great investment opportunity. The situation is not so rosy, however, thirty per cent of the population have been living below the poverty line for the last so many years. Ten per cent of the population are living below the critical poverty line: their income is insufficient to pay for even minimal nourishment. So much of the workforce is unemployed or under-employed.

A distinguished North American political scientist, Dr. Benjamin Barber, recently pointed out that in the United States democracy had degenerated into bringing one group of rascals in for four years, and then throwing them out and replacing them with another group of rascals for four years. From the perspective of the South, that looks very good! In a context where rascals manipulate elections and stay in power for fifteen or sixteen years, I would appreciate the chance to throw them out through peaceful elections every four years.

Thus, the complaints of the North are often the aspirations of the South. Progress in industrialised nations can be a threat to developing countries.

Ten years ago, in the euphoria of globalisation and the expansion of services and finance that followed the fall of the Berlin Wall, I advanced the idea that we were entering a fractured global order. Globalisation brings us into contact with one another, but it also strengthens profound divisions and fractures in terms of societies and income, and most importantly in our capacity to generate and utilize knowledge. Over the last ten years, the concentration of wealth and power has greatly increased both within and between societies.

There is a real risk of two civilisations emerging, with two ways of viewing and relating to the world: one based on the capacity to generate and utilize knowledge, the other passively receiving knowledge from abroad and deprived of the ability to modify it.

The world now faces the prospect of this Knowledge Divide becoming an unbridgeable abyss. We need the international community to return to the basic principles of international co-operation and introduce the idea that a minimum level of science and technological capability, including access to the internet, is an absolute necessity for developing countries and should be the subject of international solidarity.

This can be achieved. However, contrary to the situation of 20 years ago, national governments are no longer the major players in the game of science and technology. Whether we like it or not, the private sector and the international community of scholars must be invited to the table with governments from the North and South to begin discussing an agenda for the mobilisation of a science and technology for development. United Nations with a mandate for the development of the sciences, has a special role to play in the revitalisation of international co-operation in this field.

10

The Electronic Gap

In the United States, business journals, market gurus, economics professors and highly paid consultants talk incessantly about the coming global boom, the transformation of the workplace, the technology revolution and the knowledge explosion. It is implied that the world is slowly becoming a reproduction of Silicon Valley. It is asserted that this is the future. But instead of swallowing this type, perhaps we should pull back and look at the globe as a whole.

The pessimistic view would be to point out what is currently occurring in Kosovo, West Africa, Rwanda, Chechnya, Kashmir and elsewhere. We might also follow Robert Kaplan in the trips he describes in *To the Ends of Earth*, only to discover that much of humanity is headed for disaster and self-destruction. I do not wish to be as negative as that. However, I would like to offer a caution to those who portray globalisation in an uncritical and overly enthusiastic manner.

One in three Americans are regular, daily internet users. Even within American society, the computer and e-mail have widened the gap between educated people (chiefly whites and Asians) and the less educated (chiefly black Americans). This gap will be felt in every aspect of life, whether it is in opportunities, potential, education or job-hunting. The United States will be divided into two groups, one which is computer-literate and the other which is not.

This phenomenon has been replicated at the international level. The most important fact is that we are in the midst of a technology revolution that sees less likely to close the gap between rich and poor countries than to wide the gap even further.

The technology revolution and the communications revolution still bypass billions of human beings The internet may have more influence than any single medium upon global educational and cultural developments in the coming century. Yet only 2.4 per cent of the world's population is on the internet, or one person out of 40. In Southeast Asia, only one person in 200 is linked to the internet. In the Arab states, only one person in 500 has internet access, while in Africa only one person in 1,000 is an Internet user. This situation will not change as long as those lands lack electricity, telephone wires and infrastructure. They cannot afford either computers or the expensive software they require. If knowledge indeed equals power, the developing world may have less real power nowadays than it did 30 years ago, before the internet was developed.

If we want to work toward a knowledge-based society in the coming century, over at least the next 10 years we need to make a concerted effort to bring poorer societies into the system of electronic communications. This effort will need to be coordinated by the World Bank, the UN Development Programme, UNESCO, the NGO community and the global business community.

The alternative is to perpetuate a world fundamentally undemocratic and structurally unsound. If we do nothing, if we let the knowledge explosion intensify in technology-rich societies while poorer societies fall further behind, the growing gap between haves and have-nots will lead to widespread discontent and threaten any prospect of global harmony and international understanding. This is the most significant challenge we face. We have no time to waste in responding.

11

Net Gains or Net Dreams?

What is knowledge-intensive development? Can the internet support it? Will this support make any difference to the lives of people in developing countries who are disadvantaged or marginalised? How can governments and other stakeholders ensure that their societies benefit from the new network technologies and services? This paper probes key implications of knowledge-intensive development and the internet. The new information networks can help, but governments and other stakeholders must introduce new policies to dismantle barriers.

Never before has so much chatter been heard in policy and business circles as well as in citizens' and ethical interest groups about the impact of advanced information and communication technologies (ICTs) on the global economy and the social order. For developing countries, these impacts are hard to track because of the rapidity of technical change and the unevenness of network and service availability. Education, training and skills development are failing to keep pace with the spread of the new ICTs, a growing source of anxiety for people in developing countries. Research is yielding contradictory evidence about who will benefit and how. The Global information Infrastructure is penetrating the developing world and making claims on limited investment capital. Poverty, illiteracy, poor health, under-funded education, and worsening environment conditions are also making big claims on public resources. Everyone hopes that digital ICTs and the arrival of the vast networking potential of the internet will help remedy these ills.

The new ICTs are opening access to a flood of information from local and global sources. Converting this information into solutions to high priority development problems is the big challenge. The potential of ICTs must be harnessed to achieve major social and economic benefits. In principle, new digital networks and services could be used to communicate more quickly and cheaply, bringing the village to the world and the world to the village. The vision is one in which inclusion of people in developing countries in a more knowledge-intensive development process follows from access to services like the internet.

'Net' visionaries portray a world in which access to the internet and other information and communication services is all that matters. They acknowledge risks for people in developing countries, but they move on quickly to promote the use of new products and applications which, more often than not, have been designed in ignorance of development realities. The globalisation of markets for technologies and services, the rise of dominant firms like Microsoft, the emergence of a handful of global telecommunication operators, and increasing shortages of skills in key areas, mean that neither the benefits nor the risks of these technologies can simply be assumed. Harnessing networks and services to deliver benefits in developing countries means ensuring that those facilities are responsive to the poorest and most disadvantaged groups and communities. It means experimenting with new partnerships that boost equity, mobilise investment for building capacity and spur the harvesting and sharing of scientific and technical knowledge. It also often means pushing for national or regional participation in the global governance systems that steer trade, regulation, and intellectual property and privacy protection.

The new networks and services offer fresh opportunities for global and local change. But too much focus on the technical aspects of electronic commerce and new social applications means that organisational, social and cultural transformations are insufficiently heeded. Decision makers in developing countries need to take measures to ensure that ICTs can be used as 'tools' for social and economic development alike. Users need to accumulate new skills through formal and informal education, and learn how to use new sources of scientific and technical information to tackle problems creatively.

The articles that follow show that knowledge from ICTs can be converted into real social and economic benefits if new approaches like 'knowledge management' are effectively employed by governments and other stakeholders to overcome barriers. The internet is enabling research results to be shared among community workers, businessmen and women, educators, and scientists worldwide. This exchange of knowledge is sparking novel ideas about how to harness ICTs to suit development purposes.

More research is urgently needed on the way ICTs are influencing the activities of women and men, on how skills and capabilities can be built up to tackle local and national problems, and on why some initiatives to use the new technologies and services succeed while others fail. It must draw upon the experiences of people in developing countries. Studies of global market trends and structures for ICT supply are needed, to gauge opportunities for people in developing countries to develop new services for strengthening their economies, creating jobs and reducing poverty.

Although there are substantial risks, potential gains from ICTs are far greater. Governments and other stakeholders should face upto the implications of the 'IT Revolution'. National or regional ICT strategies should be set in place, corresponding to each country's development goals. They acknowledged that the next decades are not likely to see the gap between rich and poor vanish. But they argued that if governments and other stakeholders could find ways to use ICTs creatively, the gap at least could be reduced.

The social and economic exclusion of people in developing countries will not be eliminated by 'technobabble' about the Global information Society, nor by dreams of 'Cybertopia'. However, when people's creative efforts and financial resources are combined to use ICTs to encourage innovative forms of knowledge-based development, there are likely to be substantial benefits. Action must be taken to ensure that visions beget policies so that ICTs bring more gains than losses to people in developing countries.

12

Inclusion or Exclusion

Will the networked economy widen or narrow the gap between developing and industrialised countries? As we move from the industrial to the information age, access to the global information infrastructure for economies, companies and individuals becomes paramount.

The debate about the welfare implications of the information revolution 'for developing countries has' given rise to diametrically opposed views. Some believe that information and communications technologies (ICT) can be mechanisms enabling developing countries to "leapfrog" stages of development. Others see the emerging global information infrastructure as contributing to even wider economic divergence between developing and industrialised countries. The reality is more complex.

A number of trends are broadly recognised as the hallmarks of the information age. *First,* ICT progress is expected to continue to promote the proliferation of communication networks as the costs of delivering these networks decline and the quality of their services improves.

Second, in a networked environment, the incentives for specialisation and outsourcing increase. This puts a premium on flexibility and responsiveness as business cycles shorten and interactions between producers and consumers expand.

Third, electronic commerce is expected to continue to expand rapidly and further contribute to the internationalisation of service activities.

Fourth, information flows are at the very core of the globalisation process as countries and corporations project power by promoting their own culture and values on a global basis.

These trends suggest that the countries that are better positioned to thrive in the new economy are those that can rely on: widespread access to communication networks for their companies and citizens; the existence of educated labour-force and consumers; and the availability of institutions that promote knowledge creation and dissemination.

Income Inequality and Computers Literacy Gaps

The quality and coverage of schooling at all levels are also characterised by significant gaps between industrialised and developing countries. These gaps reinforce income inequality, not only internationally, but also within each nation as the ratio of female to male illiteracy tends to be higher the lower the level of economic development and the benefits of public education are typically skewed toward the richer classes. The gaps are even more dramatic when translated to the field of computers literacy.

Finally, developing countries are ill equipped to implement pro-competitive regulatory regimes. In the same vein, the culture of protection and enforcement of intellectual property rights is often an alien concept. The same applies to reliance on networks to promote transparency and access to government services.

All these indicators seem to point towards a social transformation that will increase rather than diminish economic divergence at the international level. Developing economies would be condemned to fall further behind in the international economic race because of their lack of connectivity and ability to transform the information explosion into a knowledge revolution once one analyse the drivers of the information revolution, however, a different picture begins to emerge.

Technological developments are rapidly eroding economic and technical barriers to entry into communication networks. Developing countries can, for example, leapfrog stages of development by investing into fully digitised networks rather than continuing to expand their outdated analog-based infrastructure.

First, by developing a modern information infrastructure countries can reduce isolation and exclusion. Many countries are experiencing fast expansion of cellular telephony as an alternative to inefficient conventional network services. Wireless technology can also provide affordable connectivity to rural areas in a fraction of the time that was required in the past to expand conventional telephone networks.

Second, countries can accelerate educational development by using their information infrastructures for distance education. The costs and effectiveness of such programmes are improving dramatically. ICT is also being used for lifelong learning, opening opportunities for new players in education systems. In developing economies, the dynamism of these new entrants can challenge convential educational systems and play a catalytic role in their transformation.

Leapfrogging Stages of Development

Third, a modern information infrastructure can also be a powerful force for better governance. It can, for example, enhance tax administration, audition and control. Moreover, countries can now automate their institutions administering intellectual property rights, strengthening their efficiency and enforcement capability at a fraction of the costs that prevailed in the past.

In short, the logic of the networked economy is one of inclusion rather than one of exclusion. As technological progress continues to push the costs of computing and bandwidth down, opportunities for development-oriented applications of ICT will multiply. Moreover, for those already connected the value of the network increases exponentially as new participants join the community.

Technological Determinism and Government Policies

These considerations point toward a more optimistic scenario for developing countries' participation in the emerging knowledge economy. Although, no doubt, income and wealth inequality may increase in the initial stages of the process, catch-up can also happen at a much faster pace than in the past. ICT spending, for example, grew more quickly in most developing regions than in high-income economies in the 1992-97 period. And countries like South Africa and Brazil already boast a higher share of networked personal computers than most industrialised economies.

These scenarios can be criticised for sharing a common feature: technological determinism. The different outcomes predicted, however, illustrate that they are also influenced by other variables, in particular, government policies.

If, for example, developing countries maintain regulatory barriers to the expansion of networks—e.g., by favouring monopolistic providers for telecom services—the likelihood of the first scenario increases. In this case, global dualism will be magnified not only across the conventional North-South divide, but also in terms of country-level economic inequality as a small elite of connected people in the South benefit from the global information infrastructure.

On the other hand, if regulatory roadblocks are properly addressed and efforts to promote universal access to value-added networks and computers literacy are implemented, then the possibilities for catching up will proliferate. Participation in multilateral efforts—e.g., negotiations conducted under the World Trade Organisation and the World Intellectual Property Organisation—can also be used to leverage the process of institutional modernisation. Under these circumstances, the benefits of the revolution will be widely disseminated both at national and international levels.

The most likely outcome, however, is a combination of both scenarios in which a subset of developing countries is able to converge with high-income economies more quickly than ever before while others lag further behind. International efforts to promote pilot projects in this field can increase the number of countries in the first category.

13

Challenging Traditional Economic Growth

Today, saving the planet is about redefining our economic development models. Stirving towards the fulfilment of basic human rights is an integral part of environmental protection. Without a people-centred development strategy we will fail. Conflicting interests and lack of vision and courage are among the many reasons why it is so hard to meet needs in a world of plenty. We are faced with three major challenges in the 1990s:

- to curb population growth and poverty;
- to search for sustainable production and consumption patterns;
- to promote equity.

Population growth is often associated with poverty. But who causes the major strain on the environment? The 1.2 billion poorest people consume small amounts of the world's resources and contribute little to harmful emissions. They do not cause a heavy burden. The day-to-day struggle for survival of the poorest does, however, undermine their resources, and this causes deaths as population grows beyond the carrying capacity of nature. Here two key elements are essential: to turn from non-renewable to renewable resources, and to minimize use of resources through resource efficiency. We must single out the products and processes that must be phased out and those which may be allowed to expand. Right prices that include the ecological costs will be explored further, together with administrative measures. We are ready to examine the possibilities of using "green tax" reforms to enhance employment and harness pollution and inefficient resources use. By shifting the burden of taxes from labour to environmentally harmful products and processes we might achieve a double benefit.

Transport, waste management, energy and land use are obvious areas that need to be affected by policy changes. Individuals must use their power as green-conscious citizens and shoppers—but, in the end, producers and service providers hold the main key to practical action.

The market must be harnessed to meet people's needs both for present and future generations—starting by making economic policies play by the rules of nature. The World Trade Organisation (WTO) negotiations have provided us with instruments to regulate world trade.

Getting the Prices Right

Car emissions may be cut drastically, but the rapid increase of new cars nullifies the benefits. Even the most ardent technological optimist must admit that we need new priorities or cuts in some products and services. For example, we must improve public transport and resource-efficient cars—and reduce traffic.

Traditional economic growth models fall short of solving the problem of unemployment. Indeed, 'robots' and wasteful resource use replace people. There are great job-creating possibilities in environment-friendly produces and processes. Striving towards equity within and between nations, and within and between generations, is the major challenge of our time.

The fact that 20 per cent of the world's population consumes 80 per cent of the world's resources has too long been seen as mainly an ethical challenge. Ethics are not easily translated into politics, especially when confronted with economic and market realities. As equity gradually becomes a security issue—as it will, if we do not bridge the gaps within and between nations—it will climb to the top of the political agenda.

Many of the main conflict areas of today are battlefields of resource management. These will expand greatly if we do not turn conference statements of good intention into action. The 30-year old commitment of the rich countries to meet the target of 0.7 per cent of GNP in official Development Assistance remains unmet.

Two hundred years of Western-led development optimism reached its peak in the late 1980s. When the Berlin wall fell, the economic growth models of the rich countries had become the universal recipe. But as more and more people aspire to join the ranks of the middle classes, the resulting environmental stress calls for a halt, or a radical change of course.

The call for new patterns of production and consumption challenges our traditional concepts of economic growth and the focus on materialism in our culture. Neither the industrialised nor the poorer countries are strangers to radical process of change, though the reasons for change are shifting. And we are truly facing challenging and conflict-provoking changes.

No nation by itself can solve the problems we face. Pollution knows no frontiers, but comes to us with the winds and waves. We have become more and more interdependent. If we are to attain sustainable development, we must commit ourselves through international agreements, through an international rule of law, through the development of financial mechanisms and through institutional agreements. We must develop means and tools to enhance collective security and mutual interests.

14

Can Economic Growth Reduce Poverty? *New Findings on Inequality, Economic Growth and Poverty*

Many people still think first of 'economic growth' in relation to poverty reduction. Indeed, their correlation is one of the most-discussed issues of combating poverty. The relationship is of great importance because if there is a clear causal dependency, reducing poverty could fundamentally be limited to measures to promote growth. However, if there was low growth or stagnation it would not be possible to reduce poverty decisively. In the opposite case, that of the phenomena having no causal relation, promising measures to reduce poverty could be taken up even without economic growth.

Hardly anyone now explicitly expresses the view that economic development trickles down automatically to the poor. Practical experience has refuted this assumption dating from the early days of development policy in the 1960s. However, a number of studies show development of growth and a decline in poverty running parallel. On the other hand, there are also examples which show that despite high economic growth, poverty is not reduced markedly. The common answer to the question this raises is thus: Yes, growth can reduce poverty, but only if additional measures oriented on the poor are taken up. This is often termed pro-poor-growth. But what that means in detail, and whether economic growth as such plays a causal role at all, is not clarified. It is worth taking a look at the arguments on the basis of more recent empirical and theoretical knowledge.

No Direct Causality Between Growth and Poverty Reduction

Among the many indicators of poverty, the income of the poor (income poverty) has the closest relationship to economic growth. An increase in gross domestic product and thus national income could, if other factors come into play be linked with an increase in the per capita income of the poor.

Such a relationship between economic growth and the income of the poor, however, cannot be described as causal, as is asserted implicitly time and again by the statement that growth is a necessary but not sufficient precondition for poverty reduction. Insofar as growth and poverty reduction arise at the same time at the end of a process, they exist alongside each other. It would be almost a tautology to say that the former is the cause or part-cause of the latter. Both express the same thing, namely a change in per capita income as well, and both have similar causes. What matters is recognising what these causes are and what specific factors must come into play so that the income of the poor grows too. Growth as a "prerequisite" or "condition" is then no longer the focus; the priority is asking for specific policies that result in higher incomes for the poor. The detour in thinking about growth is not necessary. Since, however, it is based on similar factors, such as fiscal policy/budget structure, employment policy, combating inflation, and institutional development, economic growth can also emerge if poverty is reduced. The difference of views lies in the fact that under the heading 'poverty reduction' the aim is no longer growth, but a purposeful reduction of poverty.

Therefore, in reverse, successful combating of poverty can be seen as being the cause of growth insofar as activating the capabilities of the poor and using their productive capacity of the poor and using their productive capacity triggers economic drive.

Indirect Causality Between Growth and Poverty Reduction?

So even if economic growth fundamentally has no direct causal impact on poverty, growth still can reduce it indirectly. This is the case when due to positive economic development a government has greater revenue and uses the surplus for combating poverty, for example by providing such public goods as education and health services. Also in these cases, however, growth is not a compelling precondition. Even without growth greater government revenue can be achieved for example by more efficient tax collection. And leeway for social welfare spending can be gained by redistributing the budget, such as by cutting military appropriations. Furthermore, an automatic process is not given because the government can also use surplus funds for non-social purposes.

Creation of jobs due to increased economic activity can be another indirect link between economic growth and income poverty, if such a development generates income and reduces poverty. But also in this case I see no compelling causality because, for instance, industrial jobs are not necessarily open to the really poor. In addition, these positive impacts occur to a considerable extent only in the event of labour-intensive development. In many countries, however, economic growth is achieved by capital-intensive production.

Inequality, Growth and Income Poverty

If national incomes, grow, a naïve observer might assume that the income of the poor must also grow along with it. But that would be a statistical fallacy. Even if only the income of the rich grows, this results in macro-economic statistics showing a higher per capita income. What the true conditions are is shown as soon as one divides the population statistically into income groups, such as in fifths, as is usual. It then turns out that the bald figures on average per capita growth can certainly cloak a situation where the income of the richest fifth of the population is growing fast while that of the poorest fifth is stagnating. Despite growth, the gap between the two becomes even wider.

The unequal distribution of income (and of other assets such as property and access to social services), and its connection to poverty reduction and growth has recently returned to the forefront of the debate.

It is obvious that inequality and its changes have direct effects on the poverty situation. Does inequality also have an impact on poverty via its relation to growth, because growth promotes or reduces inequality? Earlier, the predominant view was that rapid growth was linked with at least a temporary increase in inequality, so that a distinct policy of growth initially disadvantaged the poor.

The current dominant view is that growth has no foreseeable effects on inequality and that inequality changes only very slowly, in reverse, however, it is assumed that greater equality is a determinant of growth. According to that view, an indirect relationship between poverty on one side and inequality as a factor dependent upon growth on the other is not given.

That leads to the conclusion that fair distribution has more weight than growth. Fair distribution, however, does not depend upon growth. An appropriate policy is possible at any time, not only after an economic situation has improved. The notion that still shimmers through the debate that "something must be earned first before it can be distributed", is wrong. It is a matter of designing policy and the entire economic process right from the start in such a way that the surplus benefits all including the poor. Important elements of such a policy are, for example, land reform and development of finance systems.

Relationship of Growth to Poverty

According to today's conventional wisdom, income poverty expresses only a part of what poverty means. Not least through the voices of the poor themselves, it has become clear that violation of human dignity and rights, a lack of participation in decisions and exclusion from society, unequal treatment of men and women, and vulnerability are also regarded as poverty. For poverty is caused to a great degree by conflicts of power and interests. Income poverty often is not even seen as the greatest problem.

What relationship do these more far reaching characteristics of poverty have to economic growth? A direct relationship of growth to socially-related aspects such as women's inheritance rights, land rights and exclusion from decisions cannot be seen. Considerable improvements in favour of the poor can be achieved here even without economic growth.

Those who see a strong and causal connection between economic growth and poverty reduction must ask themselves what the prospects are for high growth rates and thus for a decline in poverty. Coupling poverty reduction to economic growth is problematic. If only low growth rates are to be expected.

Another question is whether continuous increases in growth are at all desirable and possible in the medium to long term. In this connection, a difference should perhaps be made between developing countries and industrialised nations. But environmental compatibility and availability of resources set limits to growth for both. Some academics assume that industrialised nations have already reached an inherent limit (stagnation theory) and that the high growth rates of earlier years will not return. Moreover, they add, full employment is no longer achievable due to, among other things, an ongoing increase in productivity, and current unemployment cannot be reduced by customary means. In any case, if growth were to be taken as the major benchmark, the prospects for a radical reduction of income poverty around the world would be modest.

Summing up

Poverty is a complex problem and reducing it depends upon many interconnected factors that is why poverty cannot be attributed to one main cause nor its reduction based on one main strategy. Economic growth is just one strategic element among many others related to poverty reduction. An indirect causal connection between growth and poverty reduction can only be seen because governments will have a grater scope for action due to economic growth, and if they promote labour-intensive development.

Therefore growth's role in poverty reduction must be put into perspective growth cannot be the first thing that comes to mind, nor is it the golden path to reducing poverty. The simplistic theory of economic growth as the main condition obstructs the bigger picture; it clings to the underlying and ongoing belief in the trickle-down effect. Even if there is no growth or for inherent reasons there can be none, there are promising ways to take on the challenge of mass poverty in the developing countries. Up front, governments and bilateral and multilateral donors must have the political will to design economic, financial and social policies so that they are oriented on poverty in a coherent way—the result can also be economic growth.

15

Development Requires More Ownership

To achieve lasting economic growth and a substantial reduction in poverty, developing country ownership needs to be successively strengthened. The international debate on what constitutes the right economic policy for development has become considerably more intense in recent years. Some of the recommendations that prevailed in the 1980s and '90s, based on neo-classical economic theory, had to be revised. Central to the economic recommendations of the 'old' Washington Consensus were liberalisation and deregulation of the economy as well as 'neutral' monetary and fiscal policies.

With the Cologne debt relief initiative the Washington consensus and its structural adjustment strategy were basically relegated to the past. They were superseded by the concept of Poverty Reduction Strategy Papers (PRSPs). This approach depends on developing countries drafting policies themselves ("ownership") with the involvement of civil society ("participation"). So far, however, the international financial institutions have neither thought to the new concepts through to their conclusion nor placed them in a coherent context. Several conceptual gaps still remain.

It is still largely unclear how forces can be mobilised for growth in developing and transition countries and how their economies might be better shielded against external shocks and instability. In the light of current trends, it is feared that many countries will hardly achieve the Millennium Development Goals (MDGs) unless sustainable economic growth is attained and harnessed to reduce poverty.

This suggests that donors have not adequately implemented the new approaches yet. While the Bretton Woods institutions have introduced sweeping reforms—the World Bank has acknowledge the key role institutions and "governance" play in development and has replaced its purely market based approach in favour if more practical solutions—discrepancies between vision and reality persist on the ground.

Shortcomings of the Washington Consensus

Some of the shortcomings of the old policy recommendations are well known. They ignored distribution issues, for example, paid little attention to the role of institutions, and assigned only a passive role to macro economic management. The neo-classical equilibrium model on which the Washington Consensus is based permits analysis of allocation aspects but does not take institutional or socio-economic structures into account. The "Standard Packages" of structural adjustment programmes were usually far less differentiated than the related political recommendations in general. Core elements of the programmes were swift privatisation and liberalisation of capital markets. Deregulation and liberalisation were deemed adequate requirements for optimising resource allocation and paving the way for high growth.

Efficient institutions curb insecurity and thus increase readiness to invest. Long-term maintenance of dynamic growth processes is possible only where there are institutions, which help boost productivity, guarantee a high degree of stability and reduce vulnerability to external shocks.

Unconventional Approaches

Such findings need to be properly thought through and translated into action. This means actively helping developing and transition countries to plot their own course. It also follows from the paradigm shift marked by PRSP that donors should accept unconventional policy measures. "Ownership" means donor institutions, should open to alternative economic policy options, including macro-economic options. Without diversity at concept level it will not be possible to mobilise sources of growth on the requisite scale.

The discussion paper makes a number of general conclusions: relating to economic policy. They particularly concern the quality of institutions, regulatory systems and governance and the issue of property rights, which needed to be seen as factors fundamental to all other forces for growth. These issues should systematically be taken into account when economic reforms are drafted. This is especially true for reforms based on liberalisation and privatisation. If necessary, liberalising action should be postponed until the minimal requirements are met in institutional and macroeconomic terms. The question of time frames for reform should also be given serious consideration and not-as is often the case-dismissed as a mere detail of "timing and sequencing".

There is no universal recipe for development. Solutions need to be customised and country-specific. It is important that reforms should be anchored in the political, economic and cultural landscape of the developing country in question and that its financial and administrative capacities ought to be taken account of. Feasible reform needs to be given higher priority then ideology. Second-best or even third-best options are generally better than "pure doctrine" if they suit the context of the country.

More attention needs to be paid to the question of dept sustainability Financial transfers—and especially Overseas Development Agency (ODA) loans—need to result in more investment and higher productivity. Situations where countries amass unsustainable mountains of debt need to be prevented to reduce susceptibility to external shocks. ODA should take account of individual countries' situations. This calls for more flexible, more adequately tailored financing instrument For MICs, the structure of external debt is also significant: short-term volatile currency transfers are particularly problematical.

Confining Conditionality

To increase long-term growth and to substantially reduce poverty, developing country owership needs to be successively strengthened. Primary requirements are:

- better use and targeted development of local analytical capacities (for instance through Poverty and Social Impact Analyses—PSIAs);
- advice by external partners (especially the Bretton Woods institutions) on a wide range of policy options including unconventional policy proposals;
- no taboos concerning macro-economic issues, they should be included in the PRSP process; and
- geater cofinement of World Bank and IMF programme conditionalities to core areas.

Better safeguards should be provided against external shocks. The lending policy of multilateral and bilateral donors needs to be adjusted to suit the debt sustainability of recipient countries in this context, it is important to (continue to) develop financing facilities, which allow swift assistance in the event of external shocks. At the same time, financing instruments need to be designed to reduce debt-servicing risks. Examples could be government bonds with interest payment tied to GDP growth or more flexible arrangement for the servicing of concessionary credit. To eliminate exchange rate risks, more ODA loans should be denominated in local currencies.

The World Bank needs to strengthen its strategies for crisis prevention and, in particular, for dealing with external shocks and managing crises.

More account needs to be taken of macro/micro-level interaction. Efficient strategies for promoting economic growth and reducing poverty are possible only where macro and micro policies are functionally interwoven.

Last but not least, PRSP processes need to be improved and poverty reduction and other development strategies made more explicit. It is a well-known fact that many PRSPs do not adequately define priorities, identify trade-offs between the different goals and measures or signal the budgetary implications of the measures that are planned. In particular, they generally fail to make any mention of potential sources of future economic growth, let alone craft strategy for mobilising them. Only when these shortcomings are eliminated can PRSPs become real planning tools.

16

Migration and Development

Migration and development is a growing area of interest. There has been much debate on the negative impacts of migration on development and vice-versa. On the one hand, it is argued that underdevelopment is a cause of migration, and on the other that migration causes developing countries to lose their highly skilled nationals.

While there is a measure of truth in each of these assertions, properly managed international migration holds enormous potential for the development of countries. Remittances have become a prominent source of external funding for developing countries that surpass official development assistance. In 2005, over US $ 100 billion were sent home in remittances by migrants, helping to sustain the economies of many developing countries. The total amount of resource remitted may even be two or three times higher, since a large number of transactions are carried out through informal channels. Migration can thus contribute to the reduction of poverty at the local and national level, and to a reduction in the economic vulnerability of developing countries.

Migration may be detrimental to the community of origin if the labour market is depleted by the departure of its most productive and/or qualified members ("brain drain"). However, migrants who have developed and improved their skills abroad can be actors of the "brain gain" by transferring and infusing knowledge, skills and technology into their countries, of origin.

In addition, remittances sent home by migrants can be used to sustain development. The challenge is to develop mechanisms to mitigate as much as possible the negative effects of "brain drain" and to encourage the return of qualified nationals resulting" brain gain"

It should also be noted that in a globalised world, migration is increasingly circular. While many migrants still make a permanent move with their families, an increasing proportion of migratory movements are temporary in nature. Increasingly, countries of origin expect migrants to maintain financial, cultural and sometimes political links with their home country, which may be difficult to reconcile with the expectation for migrants to integrate, on the part of the host country.

In order to benefit from remittances, skills transfer and investment opportunities, it is necessary to create and maintain links between migrants and their potential by encouraging them to contribute human and financial capital to the development of their home communities.

Through advances in communications technology and the decline in travel costs, globalisation has made it easier for migrants to stay in contact with their country of origin and to establish lasting links with diasporas and transnational networks.

In the past, states and the international community formulated and implemented separate policies on poverty reduction, globalisation, security, refugees and migration, with sometimes different or even conflicting objectives.

Better results can be achieved by considering the close interrelationship between migration and development on national and international levels through coherent and coordinated development and migration polices, and between humanitarian assistance and development assistance. Migration polices dealing with the migration-development nexus include facilitating voluntary return and reintegration, either temporary or permanent, particularly of the highly skilled. Other policies address the transfer of remittances, the reduction of transfer costs and investment in the country of origin by diasporas and returning migrants.

It is also necessary to promote and enhance dialogue and cooperation and the national level between different government agencies as well as at the international level. The aim is to ensure that migration contributes to sustainable development, and that in turn development endeavours to contribute to the management of migration.

In recent years, migration has been making its way steadily to the top of the international agenda, and now calls insistently and urgently for the attention of all governments, regardless of their past involvement or interest in the management of migratory processes.

Migratory flows today are more diverse and complex, with more temporary and circular migration. World demographics, economic, political and social trends mean that governments and societies will need to put more emphasis on migration management in all of its dimensions.

If properly managed, migration can be beneficial for all states and societies. If left unmanaged, it can lead to the exploitation of individual migrations, particularly through human trafficking and migrant smuggling, and be a source of social tension, insecurity and bad relations between nations.

Effective management is required to maximize the positive effects of migration and minimize potentially negative consequences. It is essential to establish orderly and safe migration opportunities while ensuring respect for the integrity of national, sovereign borders. Migration management strategies need to result in the implementation of policies; laws and regulations that take into account the rights and obligations of migrations as well as the social and economic interests of nations and responsibilities of governments.

Over the past decades governments have tended to focus on isolated elements of migration and have thus developed ad-hoc strategies to protect their interests. For some, labour migration needs have predominated, for others asylum has been the main concern. However, to be effective, migration management strategies need to address migration in a comprehensive manner. Governments over the past decades have tended to focus on isolated elements of migration. The challenge today is to shift from an isolate and largely in effective focus to more meaningful, constructive and comprehensive approaches.

At the same time, it is necessary to identify, define and address the fundamental policy issues in the migration debates. This is a tall assignment, since the migratory landscape is complex and rapidly evolving, with challenges emerging at every step of the way.

Most governments are just beginning to develop coherent and comprehensive migration management strategies. There is still a need to better understand migration interests and priorities and to develop a common migration language. Regular dialogue between governments that allows an exchange of experience and the development of new initiatives and approaches to migration management is therefore essential.

17

Economics and Sustainable Development

Economists and ecologists were once seen as enemies: environmental protection, it was thought, could only be achieved at the expense of economic growth. The misconception persists at the extremes among both the most fundamentalist Greens and the most ideological free marketers. But increasingly it is now being recognised that development and care for the environment go hand in hand. This interdependence is coalescing in the new and necessary discipline of environmental economics.

Conventional economics patterns have often assumed that growth and technical progress will nullify all resource and environmental limits. Environmental economics recognises that the world's natural capital underpins all development, and that it is rapidly becoming scarcer as human demands exceed the globe's long-term carrying capacity. Government of India has introduced environmental measures over the last two decades, but need to move further towards integrating them into economic policies. There can be no real sustainable development unless environment and development policies are integrated at the very beginning of the decision-making process.

Quantifying the Environmental Cost

One of the first steps is to work out the true costs of polluting and depleting the world's natural resources, such as its soil, air and water, the climate and the ozone layer. These have often been regarded as free goods, and it was believed that the world has an infinite capacity to absorb the effects of human activities. Environmental economists, recognising that the social and economic costs of degradation are very great, are trying to quantify them. They say that this will make possible better use of such tools as cost-benefit analysis, environmental impact assessment and risk assessment—and the production of national income accounts which reflect the depletion an degradation of natural resources. As these costs are identified and quantified, economic policy can increasingly be developed with sustainable development as the primary objective. Achieving sustainable development requires industrialised and developing countries to make dramatic changes in national and international policies based on a global partnership. The greenhouse effect, the destruction of the ozone layer, the extinction of species and contamination of the oceans, and other environmental problems, affect us all, no matter which corner of the globe we inhabit.

The first and essential step in overcoming a difficulty is to recognize it and understand it. Concern over the difficulties related to sustainability has led scientists and national and international institutions to study the concept and suggest ways of meeting its many requirements. Indicators have been established to measure pollution levels, soil erosion, salinisation, deforestation and a host of environmental problems. Evaluating the impact of such natural resource-use on eco-systems is a major step towards finding the necessary solutions.

For example, it has become clear, on a macro-economic level, that national accounting systems fail to reflect these effects adequately, Deterioration of the world's rivers, land degradation, air pollution and contamination of the seas are not taken into consideration. Inadequate accounting distorts reality and gives a false idea of the true consequences of growth and production.

On a micro-economic level, much is being done to redefine production costs. Incorporating the cost of waste management and internalizing negative external impacts within production prices are beneficial aspects of the economics of sustainability.

Steps are being taken to evaluate public and commonly held assets and to put a price on them, even though they may not be subject to market forces. These are only in the earliest stage but they will allow for more accurate evaluation of the world's natural capital. Fiscal, market, quota and other instruments are being developed to enforce change in the way in which certain resources are used. Examples include markets for transferable emission quotas or compensatory taxation mechanisms designed to ensure that economic forces act to reduce greenhouse gas emissions. Efforts at impact analysis—and in a general sense, cost-benefit analysis—permit rough estimations of the impact that projects might have on eco-systems.

Long-term Repercussions

These instruments carry significant limitations but they are important nevertheless because they attempt to quantify impacts on the natural world and to achieve a more rational use of natural resources. The development of such instruments and evaluation techniques will have significant repercussions in the formulation of sustainable long-term policies. But we must bear in mind that sustainability is not just an economic issue: it is also a political and cultural one.

The concept of sustainability demands as alternative view point in which humankind and the natural world are perceived as a unit—as different yet mutually sustaining aspects of a whole. This perception is not incompatible with progress. It does not renounce development. It simply seeks to affirm life and refuses to discriminate between the means and the end. It understands that happiness cannot be achieved by destructive means. The questions of how to produce and how to consume therefore become extremely important. Neither should be at the expense of the future or of the natural world. Efficiency is not limited to the links between investment, products and prices: it must address the rational use of resources, including environmental and cultural consequences, both in the long- and the short-term.

Very considerable adjustments must be made in the interests of sustainable development. They demand a reassessment of all our activities which cannot, logically, be done overnight. It is a long and continuous process, characterised by steadfastness and compromise.

18

Elitist Public, High Growth Rate

The internet is changing the face of journalism. Increasingly media organisations in Asia, Africa and Latin America are posting their publications on the web. Proffessional standards are rising, because international comparison has become possible at the click of the mouse. The internet is serving democratic discourse as civic organisations maintain their own websites.

There's no doubt that many developing countries have very limited access to the web, That is no different in Vietnam where many villages are still not connected. But the speed of for expansion is astounding. Internet cafes are presently only an urban phenomenon, but they are making access to cyber world increasingly affordable. An hour's surfing cost only about 20 cents, barely twice as much as daily newspaer. And prices are likely to drop further.

Many media houses in the developing countries are already on the net or at least working towards it. Although an internet presence is expensive and doesn't normally add up in economic terms, what matters is the image gained. Many media makers in poorer countries are not even aware that most journalistic websites in OECD states are equally unprofitable. They exist because they have become indispensable from the piont of the view of profile.

- In fact the internet plays a special role in the lives of expatriate communities. They can keep themselves fully informed on current events at home on a daily basis. This also means that expectations of journalistic reporting are raised. Journalists are now serving on an online leadership accustomed to the professional standards of the advanced countries. This clientele has many different sources of information at its disposal, leaving on the place for reporting, which is strong on rhetoric but weak on facts. Resorting to such means is easier for purely regional publications reaching a public with only limited options for comparison.

Now that the elite classes in developing countries are accessing the major world newspapers on the internet, their demand for quality reporting from journalists at home is raising. Readers know that reporters and commentators in Washington, London or Paris are far more confrontational towards the powers-that-be than is the norm in many poor country capitals with autocratic pasts (or even presents). Both the constant contact with diaspora-countrymen and the reading of internationally respected newspapers are giving impetus to demands for democratic participation.

A wide range of arguments suggests that the internet is irrelevant to society in poor countries. These arguments are certainly justified, but they do not ultimately stick. It is certainly a medium for the elite classes, and one which generally requires not only a certain financial power but also knowledge of foreign languages. It is also true that it mostly serves city-dwellers. However, prices for data services and hardware are dropping fast the world over. This results in high growth rates of net usage. Moreover, in countries with poor roads and sales logistics, newspapers too are a mainly urban medium.

Above all, educated, urban middle classes provide the decisive actors in civil or organisation. Any tool, which enables them to network effectively, is therefore of great socio-political significance. The internet is particularly relevant here, because legal and economical barriers are much lower for suppliers than in the case with conventional media. An adequate internet presence requires much less financial investment than broadcasting a radio programme or printing on a newspaper. Websites of independent organisations are. not only becoming increasingly important sources of information for journalists, but publishing their www-addresses can raise the practical value of conventional media.

All this implies that media makers must up-grade their skills. This involves more than simply learning how to use various computer programmes. They must also come grips with web-based forms of presentation. Readers equipped with a mouse and monitor develop different habits than do newspaper readers in armchairs. Whether text images or sound are required, the best online-journalism has its own stylistic devices—such as interactive opinion polls. Journalists will increasingly have to master these tools, wherever they may be based.

19

Technological Entrepreneurship

The New Force for Economic Growth

Entrepreneurship has emerged as a major new force for change. The dynamic role of modern small business in economic growth has received fresh recognition worldwide. It is essential to promote entrepreneurship and to mobilize the dynamism of the private sector for accelerated national development. An unbridled private sector may not, however, ensure growth with equity. It is the prime responsibility of governments to create policy frameworks that enable business to apply technology for competitive advantage and for the well-being of the public.

The Changing Global Environment

As agents of change and progress, entrepreneurs start by identifying a market opportunity and matching this with social or technical innovations. They then proceed to mobilize the resources necessary to drive their business concept to its commercial realisation. The development of a product or service with a high-technology content—never easy anywhere, or at today's rapidly-changing global environment. It calls for restructuring the available technology and business development systems and developing the skills needed by a new breed of "techno-entrepreneurs" to transform innovations into market opportunities at home and abroad. It also requires reorienting the present processes and priorities of technical and economic cooperation among countries.

Amidst the global concerns of environmental preservation, poverty elimination and social development, the practical problems of entrepreneurship are not being properly addressed, even though entrepreneurs will create the bulk of enterprises, jobs and wealth.

A torrent of technology-based goods hits the market every week, ostensibly improving the quality of our lives while simultaneously creating complexity and dislocation. The pace of progress in information technologies, micro-electronics, robotics, new materials, bio-medical sciences, space science and other advanced technologies quickens, significantly changing the way we live. The growth of markets for these technologies also proceeds apace.

Further, technological change is taking place today against a background of growing intra-national and international disequilibria. While the transformation from state-centred to market-oriented development is opening up enormous opportunities and options, it has also caused severe short-term hardships. In order to survive and prosper in these changing times, India and its enterprises need enlightened government policies, good technical infrastructure and strong cultural roots.

Traditional production factors are giving way to a new paradigm characterised by new patterns of trade, investment and employment, and by informal networking life-long learning and technological entrepreneurship. The manufacturing sector in India continues to be dominated by food products, textiles, chemicals and other traditional industry, mainly in the public sector. However, change is coming, albeit slowly. State enterprises are being corporatised pending privatisation, and the share of knowledge-based and information-related activities in the marketplace is rising perceptibly. Restructuring policies now place emphasis (often purely rhetorical) on the role of the private sector. The legacy of decades of centrally-planned development is generally inimical to private enterprise. In turn, the private sector has been slow to respond to economic liberalisation in India and generally failed to generate the new employment necessary to absorb new entrants to the labour force.

The regulatory problems of an onerous tax structure and administration, poor access to finance and raw materials, over-regulation of labour and land use, pervasive bureaucracy and restricted markets have been significant barriers to entrepreneurial growth.

Towards Competitive Performance

The imperative of improved performance has serious implications for India if it is to survive, stay abreast and succeed. It calls for national efforts on systemic efficiency and productivity growth, the move from an investment-driven to an innovation-driven economy and sustained higher-order competitiveness; towards enhanced customer satisfaction at home and penetration of selected markets abroad. Concurrently, governments and business have to address such intractable problems as poverty, corruption and the degradation of the environment.

Creating New Technology-based Ventures

Starting a new business in India is a hazardous task. Problems are compounded when the venture is technology-based:

- Capital requirements are generally larger, while traditional banks are ill-equipped to process the perceived risk. Venture capital generally only becomes an option when the venture has documented the merits of its management, market and innovation;
- Knowledge-based ventures can benefit from linkages to sources of knowledge—e.g. the technical university or research lab. Such mentoring needs to be cultivated;
- Techno-entrepreneurs often have technical skills but usually lack the business management and

marketing skills necessary for success. These need to be supplemented;

- In fields where technology is changing rapidly, it is often advantageous to make technology-acquisition arrangements. Sourcing such innovations, negotiating technology licensing agreements and protecting the intellectual property itself require special skills;
- Knowledge-based innovations are inherently more risky than others. The management of this unique risk requires assessment techniques and vision;
- Technology-based ventures often have social and environmental implications, which need to be managed carefully;
- Penetrating a competitive market requires good market intelligence, a good strategic plan and good luck.

Special Characteristics of "Techno-entrepreneurs"

The popular misconceptions are that techno-entrepreneurs are born, not made; that they take risks with other people's money and fail more often than they succeed. In fact, entrepreneur skills can be identified and developed. The entrepreneur is typically an innovator who formulates new solutions to existing problems, mobilizes resources and stimulates others to participate in his or her team. These aptitudes develop over time, often starting in childhood, as the person faces new challenges and learns from failure.

Entrepreneurial opportunities can be found in every industrializing country, community and family. Principal sources of entrepreneurs for knowledge-based ventures are often the university and government research laboratories, the large industrial and military establishments and professional service firms. Some motivations of the entrepreneur are the need to: be independent; create value; contribute to society; earn recognition; become rich or; quite often, simply not to be unemployed. Value-adding ventures with good growth potential can best be developed in an open market and in a culture which supports risk-taking.

The techno-entrepreneur anywhere has the challenge of moving a concept through the prototype and production phases towards creation of a product which meets market needs at a price consistent with the value created and with the ability of customers to pay.

Equally important, the market itself has to be developed and sustained. It is not enough to be first with a better mousetrap if one does not have the skills to educate and reach potential buyers and to set the market standard.

Hence one has to distinguish between innovators and inventors. The inventor is typically a creative person in a quest for knowledge or for producing new products, without determining in advance whether a real market exists for his or her inventions. On the other hand, the innovator draws on existing knowledge and the talents of others to develop or adapt a product or service at a volume and cost that can capture a significant portion of an identified market. The flexibility and creativity of a small entrepreneurial techno-venture may lead to more incremental and break-through innovations than can be generated by larger-sized firms in many sectors.

The pace and pattern of India's economic development now depend in large measure on its technical resource base. In this context, the key determinants are the skills to apply technology for enhanced competitiveness, as well as to create techbased ventures. Techno-entrepreneurs have to be supported by appropriate national structures and international linkages if they are to survive and flourish in an intensely competitive world.

20

Aid Effectiveness as a Multi-level Process

Parallel to the widespread decrease of aid resources provided by donor countries to developing countries in recent years, debate and research on how to make aid more effective has become a major concern. Usually, it is suggested that decades of development assistance have at best produced marginal results in terms of improving development levels in the South. Little mention is made of donor's policy shortcomings and the negative impact of these on efforts aimed at reforming and redefining development cooperation in order to enhance aid effectiveness. The policy parameters and operating frameworks of existing aid policies continue to inhibit higher degrees of aid effectiveness. In many donor countries, opinion polls indicate waning public support for development aid.

Increasingly, the moral case for aid is called into question and deeper world market integration tends to be seen as the panacea to continued economic decline and social destabilisation in the South. Against this background, cooperation between donor and recipient actors is faced with a duel uphill struggle. First, fewer resources can be mobilised to meet growing developmental needs. On the other hand, to organise and manage development policies and programmes in a result-oriented manner, grows more difficult. The threat of further aid cuts and of further drops of public support for providing aid become ever more real. A closer look at the organisational complexities and political constraints under which development cooperation is expected to perform effectively may help to improve current aid management approaches.

Towards Conceptual Clarity

At first sight, catchy definitions of what constitutes effective aid might appear attractive to use, in particular with regard to economic indicators. The term "aid effectiveness" is easily used in the same vein as "efficiency", "significance" or "impact" of aid. At times, obsession to measure and demonstrate the results of aid supported development processes can be observed among policy-makers and administrators on the donor side. Still the understanding of aid and its effectiveness as being part and parcel of a cooperation relationship between donor and recipient side parties, is scarcely embedded in practice. To determine how to make aid more effective requires more than a quick impact analysis of an individual and perhaps even isolated development project. Consequently, defining the concept of aid effectiveness needs to take into account at what levels cooperation is focused on. To strive for sustainable and effective modes of development cooperation will entail the need to combine recipient ownership of the development process with donor accountability concerns.

Performance expectations cannot be exclusively placed on the recipient while donor interests, their aid management systems and procedures remain unchanged.

An extended and more analytical, process-oriented definition should take into account four main aspects of aid effectiveness:

(a) Effective aid must relate to the building and/or strengthening of in-country aid management capacity;

(b) To maximise the degree of aid effectiveness, local ownership of the aid process is essential: from setting of priorities through policy formulation and implementation on to the evaluation stages of the process;

(c) Increasing recipient side capabilities to take charge of aid relationship, will need to be combined with arrangements to meet legitimate donor accountability concerns;

(d) Aid effectiveness is a two-faceted objective: its realisation is equally dependent on increased transparency of donor motives and on dropping of non-developmental, political and economic aid objectiveness of donors.

In addition a broader range of stakeholders in the aid relationship needs to be actively involved: extending beyond accountable government and implementing agencies, to include democratic institutions and organisations of civil society and of the private sector.

Applying any definition of aid effectiveness without disaggregating macro-economic data and taking into account country specificity will only lead to unhelpful generalisations about aid and its effectiveness. It would seem more appropriate to adopt working definitions against which to assess effectiveness of aid resources at a country-specific level. On such a basis one could expect to arrive at more reliable indicators of how well aid resources contribute to improving developmental standards and meeting existing needs.

From Definition to Success—Key Requirements

Having reached agreement between the recipient and donor on what should constitute effectiveness of aid is only a starting point. Embarking on democratic, peaceful and participatory patterns of economic and social development must follow: to arrive at significant and lasting improvement in many of the least developed countries will be a long-term process. This being said, it is crucial to design and implements such forms of development cooperation which involve a wide range of recipient side actors, not only from the government side but also from civil society at large. Seen as a process of increasing inclusion of intended beneficiaries of aid, the commitment to decentralise as well as entrust aid and its management grows in importance.

To fully capture Third World development realities, policy frameworks inspired by neoliberalist-type of development concepts and theories are grossly inadequate. The views and positions on aid articulated in the World Bank and the IMF, or in many if not most bilateral aid administrations in OECD countries, represent only one side of today's international cooperation, namely the donor side. The major weakness to point out with respect to this locus of debate, is a profound under representation if not even a total absence of recipient experiences and perceptions on aid in general and on its effectiveness in particular. There should be little doubt that ignoring to not actively identifying and involving such perceptions, leads to strongly donor driven aid.

To circumvent recipient side insights and views on strengths and weaknesses of aid strategies and mechanisms, will result in limited local commitment and sense of ownership over the aid process. Mutual decision-making between donors and recipients remains a rare policy approach. Aid procedures that are based on local management and less control-oriented donor roles in the aid process are still exceptions in development cooperation.

Structurally, in terms of the policy environment within which development aid is expected to function, the overriding policy framework is general based on structural adjustment policies (SAP). But the underlying conclusion made by proponents of SAPs that these policies induce aid effectiveness, has yet to be proven valid. It must suffice at this point to emphasize that there is no *a priori* relationship between world market integration under structural adjustment and sustainable development in poor countries. Aid to these countries which is solely intended to reinforce fundamentally uneven and unequal patterns of world market integration should be scrutinised critically.

Some central issues need to be addressed in the course of improving aid and its effectiveness:

- institutional dimensions of aid relationships require strong policy-attention, both on the donor and the recipient side;
- capacities to effectively identify and formulate aid priorities need to be strengthened in recipient countries;
- local capacities to sustain reform efforts must be reinforced.

Levels of Intervention

If the design of aid and the terms upon which it is provided to a developing country are largely determined by the donor, the aid relationship can be characterised as essentially hierarchical. Recipient side views will rarely surface, as they are either not identified, or not well formulated. Possibilities of a recipient-led development strategies can be limited. Unless scope is provided to the recipient side actors to assume responsibilities, aid effectiveness is likely to remain low or fluctuating, and the sustainability of donor aid efforts will remain doubtful.

National planning processes and courses of national development in recipient countries should be seen as most effective where they are led under local responsibility and control. To arrive at this ideal situation, gaps need to be reduced and closed at the various intervention levels.

Donor aid resources provide valuable support for this process. Their effectiveness in meeting long-term objective of aid will need to be assessed on the basis of how well they perform at the different levels. Individual donors will expectedly perform differently at the various levels. What will prove to be the ultimate test for effectiveness is how well the donor aid performance accomplishes the broader objectives of development cooperation and how well it includes sustainable results.

In the analytical frameworks outlined here, development cooperation would seem to be confronted with the effectiveness gaps at the:

- *Structural Level:* International trade and investment patterns, debt problems and world market integration process appear as long-term constraining factors upon aid and its effectiveness;
- *Policy Level:* Dialogue and partnership in development cooperation are instrumental factors in recluding planning and co-ordination gaps with regard to policy analysis and formulation;
- *The Institutional Level* is where pertinent capacity gaps exist: capacity development efforts of donors and technical assistance measures play an important role in addressing weaknesses in aid effectiveness within a country's institutional setting;
- Finally, at the *level of aid projects* (programmes), it is generally the lack of sustainability of aid interventions which causes development activities to falter once donor support decreases or stops. In addition to technical cooperation, financial and material inputs serve to maintain project momentum and goal realisation. The issue of how to develop local capacity sufficiently in order for indigenous organisations to continue project activities initially supported by donor aid, remains the most important issue to address at this level.

Fostering Aid Effectiveness

Donor and recipient development efforts are too often isolated from one another, or poorly coordinated. They fail to address managerial and implementation bottlenecks. Cross-sectorial linkages, as well as inter-disciplinary approaches to aid problems are only slowly gaining ground. It is increasingly obvious, that decisions on aid issues are subjected to concerns outside of the responsible ministry:

finance ministers, and unfortunately even defence ministers have a strong say in how much aid is to be provided, where it is to be concentrated and under what terms to be utilised. Inside of recipient countries, large portions of national budgets are allocated to non-development priorities with little or no impact on alleviating urgent poverty problems.

Development cooperation may make the biggest impact and be executed most effectively where donors and recipients agree upon multi-level aid strategies. To give an example, building a road to a remote rural area may well be done in an effective project manner. It is equally important to have a functioning transport authority in place to ensure maintenance of the roads. If this authority operates within a nationally defined infrastructure policy, best in accord with national trade and investment priorities, then the effectiveness of the project-level road building programme has a good chance of being high.

Institutional changes to set the stage for a profound reform process in development cooperation are needed. Reprioritising national budgets to reflect identified in country development needs may be one step. Setting up policy evaluation and formulation units can be complimentary measures. Deregulating markets and investment rules may serve to please donors, but dumping of cheap products which strangle local production efforts may easily result. Regional cooperation, including intensified South-South cooperation can provide some counterbalance. There are only a few areas where changes in the current system of development cooperation can occur, with a view to better manage the complexities of aid and the social, cultural, economic and political backgrounds against which they take place. The will and commitment to take policy action in both donor and recipient countries, through the broadest range of stakeholders and institutions as possible, will be the test for genuine efforts at improving development relations between North and South and organising cooperation effectively.

21

The Truth About Global Competition

The Economic Myths Behind Globalisation

Local communities everywhere are on the front lines of what might well be characterised as World War III. It is not the nuclear confrontation between East and West—between the Soviet Union and the United States—that we once feared. It is a very different kind of conflict. There is no clash of competing military forces and the struggle is not defined by national borders. But it does involve an often violent struggle for control of physical resources and territory that is destroying lives and communities at every hand. It is a struggle between the forces and institutions of economic globalisation and the communities that are trying to reclaim control of their economic lives. It is a conflict between competing goals—economic growth to maximize profits for absentee owners versus creating healthy communities that are good places for people to live. It is a competition for the control of markets and resources between global corporations and financial markets on the one hand and locally owned businesses serving local markets on the other.

Two things of fundamental importance to each and everyone of us are now very much at stake.

- Will people and communities control their local resources and economies and be able to set their own goals and priorities based on their own values and aspiration? Or will these decisions be left to global financial markets and corporations that are blind to all values save one—instant financial returns?

- Will the life sustaining resources produced by the regenerative capacities of our planet's eco-systems be equitably shared to provide for the material needs of all of us who inhabit this bountiful planet, as well as for our children and their children unto the seventh generation and beyond? Or will we allow a global economic system that is now functioning on auto-pilot beyond conscious human control to consume and destroy the eco-system and our social fabric in its insatiable quest for money?

Economists, politicians, corporate spokespersons and the media have for years been touting the benefits of the global economy. They have called on us to support trade agreements such as the North American Free Trade Agreement (NAFTA) and the World Trade Organisation (WTO) to remove the constraints of economic borders and open to everyone the opportunities of growth and prosperity in the global economy. They have promised rich rewards for those workers and communities that become successful global competitors.

Many of the most ardent boosters of economic globalisation met earlier in the year at the annual meeting of the World Economic Forum. This Forum has for years brought together top industrialists and political figures from around the world to advance the proposition that removing tariffs and other restrictions on the free international flow of trade and money is a key to creating new economic opportunity and prosperity. It thus caused quite a stir when the Forum publicly announced that economic globalisation is producing disastrous consequences that threaten the political stability of the Western democracies. Their warning bears close examination for being one of the most honest and accurate assessments of the consequences of economic globalisation yet produced by leading advocates of that process. The observation is that:

- Economic globalisation is causing severe economic dislocation and social instability;
- The technological changes of the past few years have eliminated more jobs than they have created;
- The global competition "that is part and parcel of globalisation leads to winner-take-all situations; those who come out on top win big, and the losers lose even bigger;"
- Higher profits no longer mean more job security and better wages. "Globalisation tends to delink the fate of the corporation from the fate of its employees;"
- Unless serious corrective action is taken soon, the backlash could destabilize the Western democracies.

We don't have to go far to find examples of what they are talking about and why people are getting a bit upset as they wake up to the realities of who is winning in the ruthless competition of the global economy. The disparities between the winners and losers in the global competition are becoming more obscene with each passing day.

We are coming to realize that the extravagant promises of the advocates of the global economy are based on a number of myths that have become so deeply embedded in Western industrial culture that we have grown to accept them without examination:

- The myth that growth in GNP is a valid measure of human well-being and progress;
- The myth that free unregulated markets efficiently allocate a society's resources;
- The myth that growth in trade benefits ordinary people;
- The myth that global corporations are benevolent institutions that if freed from governmental

interference will provide a clean environment for all and good jobs for the poor;

- The myth that absentee investors create local prosperity.

The Growth Myth

Our measures of growth are deeply flawed in that they are purely measures of activity in the monetised economy. Expanded use of cigarettes and alcohol increases economic output both as a direct consequence of their consumption and because of the related increase in healthcare needs. The need to clean up oil spills generates economic activity. Gun sales to minors generate economic activity. A divorce generates both lawyers fees and the need to buy or rent and outfit a new home increasing real estate brokerage fees and retail sales. It is now well documented that in number of other countries the quality of living of ordinary people has been declining as aggregate economic output increases.

The growth myth has another serious flaw. Since 1950, the world's economic output has increased 5 to 7 times. That growth has already increased the human burden on the planet's regenerative systems—its soils, air, water, fisheries, and forestry systems—beyond what the planet can sustain. Continuing to press for economic growth beyond the planet's sustainable limits does two things. It accelerates the rate of breakdown of the earth's regenerative systems—as we see so dramatically demonstrated in the case of many ocean fisheries, and it intensifies the competition between rich and poor for the resource base that remains.

This is vividly illustrated by many of the development projects in India many funded with loans from the World Bank and other multilateral development banks—that displace the poor so that the lands and waters on which they depend for their livelihood can be converted to uses that generate higher economic returns—meaning converted to use by people who can pay more than those who are displaced.

The Myth of Free Unregulated Markets

It is almost inherent in the nature of markets that their efficient function depends on the presence of a strong government to set a framework of rules for their operation. We know that free markets create monopolies, which government must break up to maintain the conditions of competition on which market function depends.

We also know that markets only allocate efficiently when prices reflect the full and true costs of production. Yet in the absence of governmental regulation, market incentives persistently push firms to cut corners on safety, pay workers less than a living wages, and dump untreated toxic discharges into a convenient river. In our present competitive context if management does not take such measures, they are likely to be replaced by the owners or bought out by someone with less scruples who will.

The Myth of Free Trade

Many so-called trade agreements, such as the North American Free Trade Agreement (NAFTA) and the World Trade Organisation (WTO) are not really trade agreements at all. They are economic integration agreements intended to guarantee the rights of global corporations to move both goods and investments wherever they wish—free from public interference and accountability. WTO is best described as a bill of rights for global corporations.

The Myth that Economic Globalisation is Inevitable

Many of the people who claim globalisation is a consequence of inevitable historical forces are paid to promote that message by the same global corporations that have invested millions of dollars in advancing the globalisation policy agenda.

The Myth that Corporations are Benevolent Institutions

The corporation is an institutional invention specifically and internationally created to concentrate control over economic resources while shielding those who hold the resulting power from liability for the consequences of its use. The more national economies become integrated into a seamless global economy, the further corporate power extends beyond the reach of any state and the less accountable it becomes to any human interest or institution other than a global financial system that is now best described as a gigantic legal gambling casino.

All over the world people are indeed waking up to the truth about economic globalisation and are taking steps to reclaim and rebuild their local economies. Such communities face basic choices as to how they will divide their efforts between competing for a share of the declining pool of good jobs that global corporations offer and working to create locally owned enterprises that sustainably harvest and process local resources to produce the jobs and the goods and services that local people need to live healthy, happy, and fulfilling lives in balance with the environment.

Our experience with the real consequences of economic globalisation is pointing to many important lessons. One such lesson is that economies should be local, rooting power in the people and communities who realize their well-being depends on the health and vitality of their local eco-system. If it is protectionist to favour local firms and workers who pay local taxes, live by local rules, respect and nurture the local eco-systems, compete fairly in local markets, and contribute to community life—then let us all proudly proclaim ourselves to be protectionist.

Such choices are not isolationist. To the contrary, they create a foundation for creative cooperation with our neighbours—whether they be in the United States or in other countries—to share experience, ideas and technology—and to join in international solidarity in rewriting the rules of the global economy to favour local over global businesses, and to encourage cooperative relations among people and communities. It is our consciousness—our ways of thinking and our sense of membership in a larger community—not our economies—that should be global.

Millions of people are also making an important discovery—that life is about living—not consuming. A life of material sufficiency can be filled with social, cultural, intellectual, and spiritual abundance that place no burden on the planet.

It is time to assume responsibility for creating a new human future of just and sustainable communities freed from the myth that greed, competition, and mindless consumption are paths to individual and collective fulfillment. It will take millions of people around the world—linked together into a powerful political coalition aimed at radical, political and economic—reform to win the war that global capital is waging against us.

22

Towards a New Policy on Poverty Reduction

In recent years, the call for the policy which enables the reduction of mass poverty in India has increased not only from scientific point of view, but also from political and practical standpoint. Mass poverty is a problem crucial not only for the people concerned, but also for the future of humanity as a whole, and one that cries out for rapid solution. Indians still have not succeeded in permanently improving the living conditions of big parts of their population. Measures in terms of economic growth expected by Indians over the past fifty years, the preliminary growth-oriented development strategies pursued hitherto have not been unsuccessful. Many poor population groups continue to be excluded from the economic growth. The "Trickle-down effect" has failed and still fails to reach them.

Marginalisation

As a result, the course development took in India led to the marginalisation of broad sections of the population. Marginal groups arose that were denied access to the development process. They are characterised by a lack of active participation (exclusion from decision-making processes) and passive participation (failure to receive goods, services and social services). Such groups found themselves in a vicious circle. Because of their marginality they achieved only low rates of labour productivity and remained poor. They consequently slipped further towards the fringe of development. The greater the progress attained by the other sectors of the economy, the more acute the marginalisation process became. The numerical increase in membership of these marginal groups was so great that in course of time they came to constitute a considerable proportion of the population.

This mass poverty is unacceptable not only from a humanitarian point of view. It also engenders problems of global dimensions. The increasing threat to the environment, a population growth stretching the capacity of the earth to its very limits, dramatic difficulties in India safeguarding food supplies, and the still unresolved debt crisis are only the tip of an iceberg that is to a large extent spawned and nurtured by mass poverty.

In view of this situation it seems paradoxical that the scientific literature related to the problem of mass poverty apparently finds it difficult to precisely define poverty, to ascertain its causes and to asses it in ethical, political, social and economic terms. The literature often states that there is neither a generally acceptable definition nor a more or less comprehensive and stringent theory of poverty. However, the lack of generally binding definitions of the concept is due not to the often cited difficulty of measuring the societal "quality" of poverty in quantitative terms. The reason is rather that both societies as a whole and individual social groups with differing values, religious convictions, ideologies and the resulting structures and functions, reach differing conclusions on where the line between "poor" and "not poor" is to be drawn. Views differ just as widely on the societal and individual salience of poverty. A generally valid concept of poverty applicable to every social context is accordingly not available.

Absolute and Relative Poverty

In discussing the problems of poverty, a distinction must be drawn between absolute and relative poverty. In the case of absolute poverty the insufficiency of resources available to an economic entity for the maintenance of physical subsistence is so drastic that the affected parties are no longer able to live in a manner "fit for human beings". In the case of relative poverty an economic entity has insufficient resources in comparison to other economic entities. This relative poverty does not necessarily mean that those affected are unable to live a life fit for human beings. It means merely that, due to the distributional structures prevailing in an economy, individual economic entities suffer deprivation to an unacceptable degree.

Poverty can be defined in both its aspects as deprivation. The deprivation can refer to various economic, social and/or political areas of human life. Poverty then means that various economic, social, and/or political needs of certain social groups are not satisfied, or are only inadequately satisfied. How drastic deprivation must be in individual cases and in what areas it has to occur before one can speak of absolute or relative poverty depends both on the observer's concept of tolerance and standards and on the given frame of reference.

The attempt to formulate an objective and generally valid definition of poverty must be abandoned. Poverty is a complex and multifaceted problem. Since it can be caused by deprivation in different areas, there are in reality different poverty profiles. The poor are, in fact, by no means a homogenous group. There is a multitude of different poverty groups with different interest and needs, such as women and children, the rural and the urban poor, members of various ethnic groups and religious communities. This can lead not only to conflict between different poverty groups but also to discord within the respective groups, hampering the formulation of consistent strategies for reducing poverty.

Varieties of Poverty

If mass poverty is to be lastingly eliminated, its causes must be recognised and purposively eradicated. This is the only way to go beyond cosmetic treatment of the symptoms to provide permanent solutions. Poverty cannot be attributed to a single cause. It can always be traced back to the aggregation of various factors deriving to a large extent from the social system concerned. The diverss contexts in which the production factors labour, capital and natural resources, technical knowledge, and the total environment relevant to development interact give birth to different "varieties of poverty". Successful projects and programmes for reducing poverty therefore require the fullest possible analysis of all the relevant elements and relationships of the concrete social system.

Other things being equal, the lower the percapita income of the population, the greater the extend of absolute poverty. Since this average income is in turn an indicator for the level of economic development, poverty can partially be explained in terms of the factors responsible for the economic underdevelopment of India. All strategies that contribute to improving the level of economic development can accordingly also provide an at least partial solution to the problem of poverty. In other words, a well-conceived development policy can at the same time be a functioning policy for reducing mass poverty as well.

Growth with Poverty

On the other side it has to be seen that economic growth is not automatically linked with poverty reduction. Historical examples of the last three decades clearly show that economic growth can go hand in hand with poverty increase. Even in cases where the above mentioned requirements of a development-promoting policy have been fulfilled, growth was accompanied by an increase in poverty due to a missing participation of broad segments of the population in this growth process. Or to formulate it more generally: Between growth and distributional justice—defined at least as reduction mass poverty—can be a target conflict which has to be solved by other measures than by additional growth politics. In fact, the more unequally income is distributed, the more probable material poverty becomes. The factors determining the interpersonal distribution structure of a country thus also contribute to explaining poverty.

For the mass of the poor, ownership of productive resources is usually limited to their own (mostly unskilled) labour. To a lesser extent they may also have property rights in land (e.g., in the case of very small scale farmer), and in material assets (e.g., simple implements). The level of education and training that determines human capital is, by contrast, usually so low that no marked improvements of their position can be expected. In most cases the poor of a society are also completely inadequately trained. With the exception of their labour, they thus dispose of no or of only very few productively utilizable resources. This is true for both the rural and the urban poor.

Their situation is made even more difficult by the fact that their resources can frequently not be used for farming or certain activities to be carried on despite adequate qualification, this can contribute just as much to poverty as repressive measures taken by big land-owners against small farmers, or the activities of criminal groups in poor urban areas. The utilisation of property rights can also be prevented by the complete absence of the additional resources (such as credits or jobs) required to carry on productive activities, or by their being available only on unacceptable conditions.

But even if the productively utilizable resources can actually be brought into use to produce goods and services, it is still not certain that an adequate level of income will be generated. At both the national and the international level, free entry to the market for the goods and services produced is not always attained. Since there are frequent legal, physical, and psychological barriers to entering the market. In some cases, certain groups are not permitted to sell in institutionally secured markets, or may do so only subject to severe restrictions in the national context, for example, ethnic minorities, adherents of certain religions, members of particular castes.

Without a doubt, the behaviour of individual groups and persons contributes to breeding or consolidating their own poverty. A decisive role is played by the relation between the culture-specific willingness to achieve, personal attitudes towards achievement and actual capacity for performance—always with reference to underlying components of poverty. However, the social systems concerned are likely to be of far greater significance in generating poverty. As a rule, the poor are a marginal group within a social system who do not participate in the political, social and economic decision-making and development processes. This marginality is not an isolated phenomenon. It is system-related and often the very rational reaction of the poor to discriminating framework conditions for their economic as well as non-economic behaviour. If the poor are not permanently to remain passive recipients of the alms of material aid, the marginalised population groups must integrated into the system. For this purpose, considerable structural and functional changes in the systems concerned are necessary, including a certain degree of redistribution of resources, of economic opportunities, and of political power in favour of the poor. The precondition for such changes is that the ruling elites realize that in the long run mass poverty must almost inevitably lead to revolution which in most cases generates dramatic losses also for the elites themselves.

The Poor Must Act

However, in India there is no or very little ability and willingness on the part of the socially dominant groups to carry out such changes to the system. Since for the foreseeable future the poor can expect no real support from the system that discriminates against them, the initiative for such changes—if one excludes the possibility of external intervention—must come from the poor themselves. They must learn to help themselves. Self-help is consequently a constituent element in poverty-oriented development strategies. Self-help measures of this sort should aim not only to improve the situation of the poor as such. They should also contribute to overall development by personal initiative. An awareness of making a real productive contribution to a society is an important factor in 'socio-psychological" demarginalisation. Such efforts at self-help should ideally develop within the group of the poor. Under the conditions prevailing in India, self-help must always be regarded as a group phenomenon and framed accordingly. Group successes generally provide the basis on which individuals gain greater opportunities to help themselves. If, however, the poor are unable to improve their situation by their own efforts, support for these efforts must be forthcoming. Such self-help support measures can be the object of a poverty-oriented development policy. They should most usefully not intervene at the level of the target group itself but—indirectly—at that of self-help support institutions, so as to avoid stifling burgeoning self-initiative efforts.

Every form of community self-help requires the participation of its members. Participation is thus not only a development instrument, but also a goal in itself, since it gives people a sense of self-respect and belongingness. It should thus be an essential component in any development strategy for reducing poverty. In contradiction to this demand, the poor are frequently treated more as objects than as subjects in the development process. The consequent lack of participation in the decision-making process can even be categorised as a primary cause of poverty. Indeed, as long as there is no genuine delegation of initiative, decision-making and implementation, democratisation will be no more than a slogan. If development is to be durable, it is essential to involve the marginalised groups in the planning and implementation of development programmes, and to give them a right of co-determination. This participation requires the poor to develop a critical awareness of their situation. They must stop accepting their poverty as more or less inevitable and adapting their behaviour to the situation. They must become conscious of their poverty and learn to regard it as deprivation. This critical awareness is the essential precondition for them being able to help themselves. Self-help and participation are thus inseparably interlinked.

Anti-poverty strategies directly addressing the target groups of the poor and which place no great value on self-help are doomed to failure in the long run. In the euphoric development policy conviction that help for self-help was the right way, it was, however, frequently overlooked that genuine self-help can only develop durably under certain minimum political, socio-cultural, institutional, and economic conditions. If such "margins for action" do not exist, the spontaneous development of self-help rapidly falls victim to the pressure of vested interests.

Gradual Approach Needed

What goals a poverty-oriented development policy would have to adopt, what strategies in reducing poverty ought to be developed, or what strategies can be successful in given contexts all depend on the concrete form taken by the circumstances as has been addressed here. At any rate, modesty is called for in this respect. However, ambitious it may sound to attempt to formulate a comprehensive policy for reducing poverty, in reality a gradual approach is to be recommended. In most cases it is expedient to restrict initial efforts to reducing material poverty, especially since theoretical knowledge has made most progress in this field.

It should always be kept in mind that anti-poverty strategies have political implications, since in essence they always amount to the redistribution of resources and political power, and the reorganisation of institutions. The less evident the impression of a "zero-sum game", the greater will be the chances of prevailing an evolutionary development vis a vis the dominant society. From this point of view, poverty-oriented development policy is always a strategy of limited conflict, and is thus always caught between the desired evolution and the risk of revolution deteriorating into chaos that seldom improves the lot of the "poorest of the poor".

23

The Future of Agricultural Trade

In the Uruguay Round, countries recognised that the long term solution for agriculture did not lie in administered prices, trade restrictions, supply controls and export subsidies but rather in open, non-distorted markets. It is the time to take bold steps toward bringing agricultural trade into the 21st century by accelerating agricultural trade reform.

There are four key areas for accelerating reforms: eliminating export subsidies; increasing market access through substantial tariff cuts and expansion of tariff rate quotas; cutting further trade-distorting domestic subsidies; and ensuring technical standards are based on sound science.

The world's farmers and ranchers are facing two difficult challenges at the dawn of the 21st century. First, they are being asked to provide more products at lower cost, higher quality, greater variety, and in a safer manner than ever demanded before. Second, they are being asked to produce this abundance on a shrinking natural resources base that is often subject to government regulations. Meeting these global challenges will require unleashing the production potential of world agriculture while practising proper environmental stewardship. The ingenuity and hardwork we usually associate with farmers will be essential to meet these challenges, but they will not be sufficient unless we further reform agricultural trade to create an environment that rewards risk and investment and encourages efficiencies.

Today's Agricultural Challenges

Farmers are responsible for feeding a rapidly growing world population. And despite progress over the years, too many people still are not getting enough food. Many countries including the United States, are working vigorously to promote technological innovations to meet the need for food and fiber in the coming years. However, as important as this work is, it is only part of the solution. These technologies and the hard work of the world's farmers need a trading environment that encourages investment and efficient production, and generates economic growth to finance production and consumption needs long-term trends in agriculture pose serious challenges for all farmers. The same technological advances that increase yields may result in lower prices. Increasing social concerns about effect of agricultural production on the environment and living conditions result in new restrictions on farm activities. As urban dwellers and industry stake competing claims for land, water and energy, many producers find their ability to farm made ever more difficult.

Two approaches to organising the agricultural economy present a stark contrast in dealing with these challenges. One model, popular in Europe and Asia, is to retain an inward-looking agricultural system focused on supply control and government regulation geared to keeping farm prices high and, since guaranteed high prices are a drain on the treasury, to controlling production. Under this approach, bureaucrats try to assess the optimal level of national production—not so little that imports are needed and not so much that excess production; must be bought at high prices and then dumped on world markets. This "command-and-control" structure stifles farmer efficiency and ingenuity and distorts world markets, especially as subsidised surpluses are regularly exported; and it does not address the challenge to farmers to produce food for the next century. It also ignores the interest of domestic consumers (who have to pay high internal prices) and producers in other countries (who have to compete with subsidised products). Of biggest concern is that the anti-market policies of this approach hamstring the agriculture sector from pursuing the technological advances needed to meet its future challenges.

Another approach is to place agriculture on a more market-oriented basis, particularly by removing trade barriers and reducing trade-distorting policies. Greater market orientation was the principle that actions agreed to in the last set of multilateral trade negotiations. In the Uruguay Round, countries recognised that the long-term solution for agriculture did not lie in administered prices, trade restrictions, supply controls, and export subsidies but rather in open, non-distorted markets. Now is the time to take bold steps toward bringing agricultural trade into the 21st century by accelerating agricultural trade reform.

The Gains From Trade

The benefit from free and fair trading of agricultural products have immediate effects on people. Eliminating trade barriers and reducing unfair competition will help ensure that farmers have incentives to produce and consumers have access to the products they desire. Liberalising agricultural trade will contribute to better resource allocation by farmers, which has conservation benefits, rewards low-cost producers, encourages efficiencies, and removes the drag on economic growth.

Opening trading opportunities also increases the food security of food-importing countries by giving supplier countries the confidence required to put more land into production and to create marketing relationships. Trade provides consumers with year-round access to a greater variety of less expensive products, while rewarding producers who are able to find and meet specific consumer demands for high-value products. In a broader context, by allowing imports that are more efficiently produced elsewhere, trade encourages specialisation in efficient agricultural and non-agricultural production.

More dramatically, trade literally saves lives. Without the international flow of food products from areas with abundant production to areas where food is scarce, many people in the world would be eating less or not at all. Trade has dynamic effects, as well, that push long-term productivity growth. For example, access to customers in overseas markets creates an incentive for technological innovation, resulting in exciting developments in improved seed varieties and production techniques. International markets also expand market outlets, raising prices and giving producers increased confidence to produce more than required merely for national needs, allowing productive farmers to not only feed their neighbours but literally feed the world.

Equally important, trade in agricultural products is becoming increasingly critical to farm and ranch incomes. Increased productivity and often times flat domestic demand increases the importance of reliable international markets. Foreign markets are not just a dumping ground for surplus products; overseas consumers value choice and quality, particularly when producers in their own country cannot meet their demands or when they are charged inflated prices. Consequently foreign and value-added agricultural producers, raising farm-gate prices and helping support the range of agriculture-related industries.

Political reality also encourages a focus on international markets; policies based on high government guaranteed prices are ultimately politically untenable because they are hugely expensive, unresponsive to the needs of customers and producers, insensitive to environmental and agronomic realities, and a shameful waste of economic assets. Rather than farming government programmes, our producers are looking for customers around the world.

While agricultural trade benefits consumers and producers alike, it is an area in which progressive reform is ardently opposed by entrenched domestic interests. Producers in some countries, cosseted by high guaranteed prices and protective tariffs, oppose any move toward greater market orientation. Intervention in the agricultural economy—measured by the Organisation for Economic Cooperation and

Development by summing price supports, direct payments, and other support as a per cent of total agricultural production—has actually increased in some countries from the levels at the beginning of the Uruguay Round. In the last set of multilateral trade negotiations, countries began the process of dismantling protection and delinking farm support from production decisions. Consequently, reforms have been undertaken by some countries.

The WTO Opportunity

The major objective in the upcoming farm talks is to accelerate the reform process initiated in the Uruguay Round. That means further substantial negotiations on tariffs, subsidies, and other trade-distorting measures so that the level and other trade-distorting measures so that the level and direction of trade are determined by market forces, not government intervention. Four key areas are outlined below:

(i) ***Export Competition:*** Export subsidies are the most distorting trade tool because the level and direction of trade is directly determined by government subsidies. Today, the European Union (EU) is the only substantial export subsidizer—nearly all other countries agreed not to use, or have only limited resource to use, export subsidies in the last round of negotiations. EU farmers, responding to domestic prices frequently twice the world price, produce more products than can be consumed in Europe, but at such high prices that they can be sold abroad only with generous subsidies. These subsidies push other competitive suppliers out of the market (which is expensive and unfair) and discourage production in countries that have a comparative advantage in agricultural production (which is wasteful and is threatening both to the environment and to future farm production needs).

In the Uruguay Round negotiations, countries acknowledged the corrosive nature of subsidies and agreed to cap and reduce their use. The upcoming negotiations should eliminate them to ensure that countries do not resort to other policy tools that allow government spending to determine winners in the marketplace. Specifically, WTO members should look closely at curbing distorting state trading agricultural export monopolies that can disguise subsidies and exert distorting market power, along with other policies used to dispose of surplus commodities on a non-market basis.

(ii) ***Market Access:*** Measures applied at the border to stop trade currently are the principal barrier to a freer and more open trading environment for agriculture. Market access barriers deny efficient producers the chance to compete in other markets and limit the variety and quality of products available to consumers. Opening markets and maximising trade opportunities are fundamental principles of WTO, and we still have a long way to go in agriculture to open markets to competition.

The Uruguay Round Agreement set agricultural trade on a more predictable basis by requiring that all non-tariff measures, such as quotas and import bans be converted to simple tariffs. While this was a necessary first step to removing trade barriers, many of the tariffs are still prohibitively high. For example, while the average tariff assessed by the United States on agricultural products is less than 5 per cent (and nearly zero for industrial products), the average agriculture tariff-rate quota (TRQ). Where only specific quantities of imports receive low duties. Many other commodities also; are subject to high tariffs.

As we start the next century, higher tariffs should not stop the flow of imported agricultural products. Where TRQs remain as a transitional step before we achieve more open trade, we expect more specific disciplines on the way in which they are administered. Similarly, we need to take a hard look at agricultural state trading monopoly. Importers; use of these state traders may have been justifiable when more restrictions allowed on farm trade, but in the tariff-only regime it is hard to see why a government needs to insert itself between an exports and an end-user.

(iii) ***Domestic Subsidies:*** Domestic subsidy programmes are often the root cause of other-distorting polices. Subsidy policies that increase domestic prices above world price levels can be maintained only if price-competitive imports are restricted. Additionally, overproduction generated by high domestic prices can be sold on world markets only with export subsidies that bring the price down to the world price. While reining in distortive domestic subsidy programmes has value in its own right for rationalising agricultural production, the WTO negotiations will focus on their trade-distorting elements.

In the Uruguay Round negotiations, countries agreed to distinguish trade-distorting subsidies (generally those linked to the production of a specific crop or related to price supports) from non-trade distorting subsidies (such as research and development, training and environmental production). The trade-distorting subsidies were capped, and the process of reducing allowable levels of subsidies began. This distinction is a good one: the nasty sort of subsidy that distorts markets and straitjackets producers should be cut, while programmes that will increase a country's ability to produce agricultural products in the next century without distorting production incentives should not be reduced.

(iv) ***Standards:*** As WTO members make progress on cutting tariffs and subsidies, the temptation increase to disguise trade barriers as health and safety measures or other innocuous-sounding "technical standards". Moreover, when regulations purportedly designed to protect heath are instead vehicles for domestic protectionism, the credibility of the entire safety apparatus of a country is put up for questioning. When good science is replaced

> by politics, the basis for sound health policy is undermined. Therefore, increasing government accountability by putting the emphasis on sound science for health standards should discipline disguised barriers to trade and strengthen health policy.

In the Uruguay Round, countries agreed to a set of sound principles: each has the right to maintain health and safety measures, but these must be based on sound science, backed by scientific evidence and an assessment of the risk, and be no more trade-restrictive than required to meet health goals. In practice, countries have found that these principles work well—bogus measures adopted without scientific basis have been successfully challenged in the WTO without sacrificing health concerns. Creating a supportive environment for the propagation of yield-enhancing biotech products also is critical for meeting the needs of the coming century.

Agriculture is Different

Agriculture occupies a special place in the national economies of most countries around the world. Farmers are responsible for feeding and clothing people. Farming also holds a powerful claim on our national cultures that calls for the preservation of rural lifestyles and values. Farm production is subject to the cruel vagaries of weather and the relentless decline in prices and increases in costs. Some people point to these factors as justifying a different treatment for agriculture in the international economy, including justifying trade-distorting agricultural policies. This is wrong-headed; societies can support farms and preserve rural communities in ways that foster choice, protect natural resources, and expand trade.

Farm production in the next century cannot afford to be trapped in a static system in which prices are determined by government mandate, production decisions are controlled by central planners, and farmers are forced to produce only for local consumers. This myopic system cannot be sustained in any important agriculture producing society. Moreover, this type of system will not meet the needs of the coming century, when we will face unprecedented consumer demand and natural resource constraints.

Instead, I look forward to dynamic world of agricultural trade in which producers, exporters and retailers apply the creativity of the human mind to the natural bounty of the earth. In this "new" world, we will produce a greater amount and variety of food than ever before, feed the coming billions, sustain our environment, and unlock economic resources otherwise stifled by moribund protectionism, ultimately raising living standards around the world.

24

Sustainable Tourism and the Environment

Tourism is high on the international agenda. The 7th session of the Commission on Sustainable Development focused on tourism and subsequently work programmes on sustainable tourism are being developed. Also the Convention on Biological Diversity is embarking on tourism programmes and bilateral and multilateral financial institutions placed tourism high on their priority lists. The UN declared 2002 as the International Year of Ecotourism and the World Tourism Organisation adopted a Global Code of Ethics for Tourism at its General Assembly, held in Santiago de Chile.

The World Tourism Organisation forecasts that there will be 702 million international arrivals in the year 2002, that arrivals will top 1 billion in the year 2010 and that by 2020 international arrivals will reach 1.6 billion—nearly three times the number of international trips made in 1996, which was 592 million.

Travellers of the 21st century will go farther and farther. The Tourism 2020 Vision forecast predicts that by 2020 one out of every three trips will be a long haul journey to another region of the world. It is expected that China will become a major force in international tourism and the WTO predicts that about 100 million Chinese will take international trips by 2020, thus putting them in fourth place in numbers of travellers after Germany, Japan and the United States. By the same time, China will attract 137 million visitors—

63.5 million overseas visitors travelled to China in 1998 and thus outrank France as the world's top destination. It is estimated that during 1999 France will receive a record number of tourists of more than 70 million; in 2007 France hopes to attract 90 million visitors. The key resource for the most popular tourist destinations is the natural environment: coastal resorts, tropical rainforests, wildlife in national parks and alpine skiresorts, all rely on a mixture of natural beauty, good weather and safe condition to attract holiday destination is landscape and natural environment, followed by climate, the cost of the journey and the historical features of the place to visit, hence, conserving the ecological integrity and environment is imperative if tourism is to be sustained.

The pressure from millions of tourists on water and marine resources, on land and on landscape, wildlife and habitat is enormous and often has devastating impact on the environment and the local population who are increasingly deprived of access to clean water and other natural resources.

In some regions, particularly in small island countries, tourism is one of the major reasons for wasting and polluting water: on average one tourist consumes at least 6 times more water than a local resident.

Major water wasters and polluters are golf courses. In many countries, golf has brought heavy ecological and social costs: deforestation, the destruction of bio-diversity and erosion; dispossession of peoples' homes and farms; over-consumption and pollution of water and very high use of pesticides and fertilisers which threaten local residents, workers, wildlife and the golfers themselves. A survey by the Japanese National Doctors Health Insurance Association has revealed that many golfers, caddies and residents living near a golf course suffer from skin inflammation, disorders of the ear, nose and throat and other respiratory illnesses to the inhalation of pesticides because up to 90 per cent of the chemicals sprayed on golf courses end up in the air. In some areas in Thailand, diseases emerged which, prior to the construction of golf courses, had not been known.

In some regions, golf courses have depleted water supply, agricultural production has come to a halt, peasants have become impoverished and forced to migrate to urban areas in search of employment. Golf courses take large amounts of land. It is estimated that each year world wide up to 5,000 hectares of forest are cut to clear land for golf courses.

Very often, the construction of golf courses forms an integral part of a comprehensive tourism project. Adjacent to the golf course condominiums and/or hotels are built, very often also a marina, an airport and a casino. Studies have shown that such a complex not only has touristic objective but is often connected to drug trafficking and money-laundering. Even the US State Department has emphasised the link between tourism, money-laundering and offshore banking.

Cruise ships are a major cause for pollution in the Caribbean, destroying maritime life and reefs by releasing waste into the ocean. Recently the Royal Caribbean, the world's second largest cruise line was fined a record sum of US$ 18 million for dumping waste oil and hazardous chemicals into the sea. The company admitted to routinely dumping wasted oil from its fleet and that it deliberately dumped in U.S. harbours and coastal areas many other types of pollutants, including hazardous chemicals from photo processing equipment, dry cleaning shops and printing presses. Some hazardous materials, including toxic solvents from dry cleaning operations, were illegally placed in the garbage aboard the ships. The material was then either incinerated on the ship or dumped in U.S. or foreign ports mixed with ordinary garbage.

It was announced that the Royal Caribbean Cruise reported a profit of US$ 338 million in 1997, a 93 per cent increase over the previous year, Carnival Corporation's Holland, the biggest cruise company with a turnover of US$ 3 billion in 1997 made a net profit of US $836 million, 25 per cent more than in 1996. Both cruise companies have recently been fined millions of dollars for dumping untreated bilge water, oil and other waste into Alaskan waters.

However, the impact of oil and hazardous waste on water, maritime life and coral reefs is devastating and all fines paid for the damage caused by the cruise ships will not revive dead corals.

A recent Green peace study on coral reefs—one of the marine world's great natural treasures—predicts that the coral bleaching which dramatically whitened many of the world's reefs last year will escalate rapidly under accepted global climate models and that the damage would wreak havoc in fisheries and tourism, disrupting the economies of many nations.

A WWF study recently published on "Climate Change and Its Impacts on Tourism", warned that droughts, rising seas, flash floods, forest fires and diseases could turn profitable destinations into holiday horror stories. The report urges the tourist industry to persuade western industrialised governments to take more concerted action to reduce their nations' carbon dioxide emissions the main cause of global warming.

The Need for Action and Education

If governments, the international community and the tourism industry want to save the world's major tourist destinations, immediate action is required. Governments and the tourism industry must abide to the principle that environmental protection is an integral part of tourism development. In order to protect the environment and mitigate the damages caused by tourism, some countries have decided to take action: The Spanish Island Minorca and the Seychelles will introduce Eco-tax on tourism. This tax will be around US $ 12 per person in Minorca and its revenues are earmarked for the maintenance of national parks and the restoration of damaged coastline. Visitors to the Seychelles will have to buy a so-called "gold-card" at a price of 100 $ which entitles unlimited access to the country; income from this card will be used for sewage management and protection of fresh water supply.

Only if tourism investor and developers:

(a) consider the natural capacity for the regeneration and future productivity of natural resources;

(b) recognise the contribution that people and communities, customs and life styles make to the tourism experience and therefore accept that these people must have an equitable share in the economic benefits of tourism; and

(c) listen to local people in the tourist destinations, tourism may become sustainable.

Education and awareness raising campaigns at all levels are therefore imperative.

25

The Biggest Industry the World has Ever Seen

The Future of World Tourism

The year 2020 will see the penetration of technology into all aspects of life. It will becomc possible to live one's days without exposure to other people, according to WTO's latest look into the future.

But this bleak prognosis has a silver lining for the tourism sector. People in the high-tech future will crave the human touch and tourism will be the principal means to achieve this.

Tourism companies that manage to provide "high-touch" products will prosper. Upscale, luxury services that pamper and spoil their customers have a bright future in the upcoming century. But WTO's report also predicts good prospects for low-budget destinations and packages. Self-catering holiday facilities, for example, which offer plenty of opportunities for socializing among families and friends. Opportunities abound at both ends of the spectrum and there will be plenty of them.

$5 Billion a Day Industry

WTO's study Tourism : 2020 Vision predicts 1.5 billion tourists will be visiting foreign countries annually by the year 2020, spending more that US$2 trillion—or US$5 billion every day. These forecasts represent nearly three times more international tourists than the 66m million recorded in 1999 and nearly five times more tourism spending, which last year topped US$453 billion. Tourist arrivals are predicted to grow by an average 4.3 per cent a year over the next two decades, while receipts from international tourism will climb by 6.7 per cent a year.

To factor in domestic tourism, WTO multiplies arrivals by 10 and quadruples receipts, which brings us to the grant totals of 16 billion tourists spending US$8 trillion in 2020.

Tourism in the 21st century will not only be the world's biggest industry, it will be the largest by far that the world has ever seen. Along with its phenomenal growth and size, the tourism industry will also have to take on more responsibility for its extensive impacts. Not only its economic impact, but also its impact on the environment, on societies and on cultural sites, all of which will be increasingly scrutinised by governments, consumer groups and the travelling public.

We hope that Tourism 2020 Vision will be more than a useful marketing tool, that it will act as a warning signal for destinations—helping them recognize the need to prepare for the pressure of growth, WTO is advising destinations to implement long-term, strategic planning and to strengthen the partnerships, both strategically and at the operational level, between the public and private sectors.

Growth of Long-Haul

Tourism 2020 Vision indicates that tourists of the 21st century will be travelling further a field on their holidays, often to China and even to outer space. The percentage of long-haul travel is predicted to increase from 18 per cent in 1995 to 24 per cent by 2020.

Tourism companies looking to cash in on this booming sector are advised to look towards Asia. China will be the world's number one destination by the year 2020 and it will also become the fourth most important generating market. Currently it does not even figure among the world's destinations predicted to make great strides in the tourism industry are Russia, Hong Kong, Thailand, Singapore, Indonesia and South Africa.

Short pleasure voyages to outer space will become a reality by 2004 or 2005, according to the study carried out by WTO Statistics Chief Enzo Pad in consultation with 85 governments and 50 tourism visionaries.

It is expected space trips will last up to four days and cost on average US$100,000. NASA, the US space agency, has recently surveyed the travel industry for interest in space tourism and some US companies are already taking reservations and deposits from private citizens hoping to become the first tourists in outer space.

But while some travellers may be suiting up for space voyages, the vast majority of the world's population will never leave their own countries, not even by the year 2020.

Only 7 per cent of the world's population will be travelling internationally by the year 2020, up from 3.5 per cent in 1996—but still just the tip of the ice berg.

European Trends

"Tourism 2020 Vision" predicts that Europe will remain by far the leading inbound tourism region as well as the main generator of international tourists. International arrivals in Europe will reach 717 million by 2020? more than twice as many as last year.

Overall, tourism to Europe is predicted to grow more slowly than the world average; at a rate of 3.1 per cent annually, though some countries will fare better than others. Central and Eastern European countries will become the new motor for Europe, feeding and being fed by other European and long-haul generating markets. Tourism to Central and Eastern Europe will grow by 4.8 per cent a year and the former Soviet Block countries will surpass 200 million arrivals by 2016—a doubling in last 15 years.

The Eastern Mediterranean countries of Cyprus, Turkey and Israel are also expected to show good growth of 4.6 per cent a year. Tourism to the United Kingdom is forecast to grow by 4 per cent annually, just under the world average. Reflecting world patterns and increasing air travel, Europeans will be taking trips more frequently and further from home. Total outbound travel from European countries is predicted to reach 771 million trips a year by 2010, again more than twice as many as last year.

Long-haul travel to countries outside of Europe will grow by 6.1 per cent a year in the upcoming decades to reach 15 per cent of all trips taken by Europeans or 115,600,000 departures. Long-haul currently accounts for 12 per cent of European outbound travel or about 42 million trips a year.

Since the typical European tourist who spends his holiday at the beach will be more frequently choosing Asian or Caribean resorts, European beach destinations are advised to orientate their product development and marketing increasingly to new tourist sources, especially Japan, the newly industrialised countries of Asia and the Americas.

Mature European destinations will have continually to strive to seek product and market differentiation to avoid a tired 'or stale image in major generating markets.

Recipe for Success

While growth of the tourism Industry will be unstoppable In the 21st century, increased benefits cannot be taken for granted. Competition among destinations will also become increasingly fierce.

The study "Tourism 2020 Vision" outlines a series of 12 mega trends that will shape the sector and offers advice on how to better compete. No destination or tourism operator can afford to sit back and wait for more tourists to arrive. They have to be won—and there will be winners and losers. To be a winner, there are a number of imperatives:

1. Development focused on quality and sustainability;
2. Value-for-money;

3. Full utilisation of information technology to identify and communicate effectively with market segments and niches.

Product development and marketing will need to match each other more closely, based on the main travel motivators of the 21st century. "Tourism 2020 Vision" calls these motivating factors the Three E's—Entertainment, Excitement and Education.

The study also highlights the importance of image in a tourists' selection of a holiday destination in the future. While an image of safety and security is already an important deciding factor for tourists, holiday makers of the 21st century will be looking for places with a trendy image.

As 2020 Vision points out, the next century will mark the emergence the tourism destinations as 'a fashion accessory'. The choice of holiday destination will help define the identity of the travellers and, In an increasingly homogeneous world, set him apart from the hordes of other tourists.

Boutique destinations and space agencies beware! You are on the threshold of meeting the 21st century tourist.

26

Foreign Aid

Giving Conditionalities a Good Name a Development Ethics with a South Perspective

If in all honesty, one acknowledges that there are world governments quite indisputably engaged:

- In acts of representation and of exploitation of their people;
- In fostering unnecessary military buildups;
- In enacting and condoning fiscally irresponsible measures;
- In taking environmentally irresponsible decisions (or allowing a laissezfaire attitude on this); and they are guilty of (or lenient about) overt corruption and other undesirable traits such as tribalism, nepotism, gender discrimination or ehnic cleansing; and are not accountable to anybody on these counts and, for this reason, are highly unpopular both at home and abroad;
- Withholding international bilateral or multilateral non-emergency assistance is justifiable in quite a few cases unless certain minimum conditions are met by such recipient governments;
- It is conceivable to impose "fair conditionalities" in a true South-South spirit as a prerequisite before

lending money or giving assistance to the above governments (as opposed to its people);

- It is further possible to set criteria, define codes and find a consensus among organisations of the South on how to apply a set of guidelines from a South perspective to appraise the credit worthiness or aid worthiness of a given regime, not being stopped by issues falsely perceived as interfering with the recipient country's sovereignty;
- It is thus perfectly thinkable to deny a helping hand to those regimes that do not help their own kin, and instead disburse that help through channels by passing government.

False Sense of Sovereignty

Accepting such a stance poses the challenge to find criteria—acceptable to the South to sort out the 'good' from the 'not-so-bad', from the 'more clearly bad' governments amongst them. Despite there being serious value judgements involved in this and despite easy accusations being inappropriately made of this being tantamount to meddling with sovereignty issues. Setting a minimum package of such criteria is not impossible. It is a way to impose national and international accountability criteria on matters of global concern, but in a South-South context.

Among other, the new package of criteria to be used will apply agreed upon international human, economic and political rights, as well as environmental conservation principles and will be used to monitor if and how the same are enforced. But this will be done using a South perspective (to be defined). The countries of the South have to act based on the notion that we are all interdependent neighbours, and it is unconscionable to believe that we can continue to live indefinitely, side by side, amidst the kind of obscene disparities in wealth and health distribution and in levels of freedom and participation that exist amongst us today. (James Grant).

There is indeed a desire and a need in the South for increased democracy in our midst. If one is to succeed in making this desire a reality, a South-centered development ethics has to be promoted that expands abilities of the people and enforces accountability on the governments of this diverse group of countries.

For the purpose of clarity one has to first differentiate among several types of conditionality:

- *IMF Conditionalities:* These imposed (or reluctantly agreed upon) conditions most often pertain to stand-by or other loans to support countries 'balances of payments (these are the well known neo-liberal, monetarist, mostly macro-economic conditionalities that are used as a threat of reducing all external resources flows leaving governments of the South extremely limited room to manoeuvre in);
- *Other Conditionalities:* Multilateral and bilateral agencies also sometimes impose conditions for development aid which they may or may not link to recipient countries fulfilling IMF conditionalities. (The World Bank almost always takes the former position);
- Then, there are conditionalities set by private or public financial institutions when countries reschedule their external debt (those are always IMF linked, are mostly coercive rather than enabling and usually result in an impossibly large number of required stringent commitments).

Note at this point that modern conditionalities are no longer confined to aid or loan giving; they are increasingly getting linked to giving or denying access to markets. (I am sure one can think of other types of or scenarios for conditionalities fitting more restricted contexts, but I am not trying here to setup a classification; such a taxonomy is irrelevant to the central argument of this article.

Need for True Dialogue

What is relevant to the argument here is that conditionalities tend to target governmental in an all-or-nothing fashion: No compliance, no money, (or partial compliance, small money and "let's see how you do....)" Not condoning the contents of such stiff unilateral conditionalities, I understand this may often be the last choice left when dealing with matters of the macro-economic steering of national economies overall. But in development aid, economic, good governance, human rights, social, environmental, disarmament or other conditionalilties do not have to be an all-or-nothing undertaking.

Genuine negotiations should be a true two-way dialogue and defending the legitimate interests of the people of the South should not be considered as confrontation by the negotiators from the North. It is conceivable that, when imposed conditionalities are not met by host governments, they option exists for donor or credit institutions to by pass the government without withholding aid to the people of those countries altogether. Some sort of "national clearing houses" for NGO funding can be set up at national level with (pooled) donor funding; foreign aid can then be channelled through such a route; sending a clear message to non-complying governments.

The way the South has been unilaterally fighting North-imposed current conditionalilties has so far been erratic and certainly uncoordinated. The South has been posing resistance to the concept as a whole and has complained about the lack of real South-North dialogue in applying conditionalities, and this is genuine, But this is a defensive strategy, more often fought by each negotiating country in isolation, in the absence of a strong common front or backing.

Defensive negotiation strategy have worked poorly with the North as a whole, especially when applying them in the absence of collective South-South support. The South, therefore, needs to set up a common-front offensive; and in aid negotiatins, this also means the South has to demand the same flexibility from the international financial institutions and bilateral donors as the one they use when dealing with difficult economic policies in the North itself.

South Concept of Conditionality to Negotiate with North

The time is thus ripe for the South to launch a counter-concept of conditionality that will lend it credibility and bargaining power when negotiating with donor/lending institutions. In essence, the South needs to be seen effectively combating and tackling—rather than condoning in the name of a non-existing Third World unity and solidarity—the most flagrant government excesses and weaknesses in its own midst. On this issue, the South needs a more convincing platform that reflects the realities of what is acceptable to its member countries in the present day and age.

When introducing counter-conditionalities as a South proposition, we have to reject all kinds of moral scepticism, moral relativism, and value neutrality coming from anywhere; we need a non-ethnocentric ethical consensus, a cross cultural moral minimum. Ethics cannot be used only when politically convenient. There is a new global consciousness even in the political life of the world: our ethical universe is thus now planetary. The radically changing circumstances we are experiencing in the world call for a reconsideration of our ethical parameters in development. This moral underpinning of development applies both to countries in the North and in the South. The South has its own duty to intervene to safeguard the elementary rights of its individuals, of its societies and to protect its environment—setting its own standards. Responsible South leaders and politicians can no longer wash their ethical hands. The tasks is not one of simply adding ethics to international politics in the South; ethics is present in the first place.

The process of setting counter-conditions has to be used by the South to gradually encode (codify) concrete state obligations in human, economic, political, environmental and other basic rights often invoked by Northern conditionalities with varying degrees of sincerity.

Position of Strength

A counter-concept will help the South to negotiate from a position of strength, taking the offensive in the fight for its own version of what in its eyes are 'fair' conditionalities (that to begin with, do not take at face value the orthodox monetary/neoliberal model of the economic that underlies Fund/Bank programmes). A new conditionality will thus consolidate the position of the developing countries as a whole and will strengthen their negotiating position vis a vis the developed countries.

We are talking here of a sort of pro-active counter-conditionality package to be used as a counter-offer or a used in more balanced negotiations with donors/lenders. What has to be attempted is to make these donors/lenders adopt the South's concerns as their own as a basis for an equal-footed partnership ("If we win, they win...") and this, requires new openings as the following counter conditionality package offers.

This counter-offer will:

- Use the South's collective influence to promote its member's interests giving them added individual moral force;
- Consider all current options and techniques in external aid negotiations to apply them as is fit to the situation in which the South finds itself today;
- Be based on the notion that development aid conditionalities are not an all or nothing proposition, giving non-governmental outlets access to the aid instead when negotiations with the governmental break down;
- Focus less on macro-economic policy reform and more on increasing the efficiency, transparency and accountability in government; it will, therefore, upgrade public bureaucracy, as well as decentralise and promote citizens organisations;

- Hold as central the concept of customised conditionally which calls for policy packages that are customised to the actual circumstances of recipient countries;
- Bargain for reverse (or reciprocal) conditionallities which, on the one hand, have to do with the decentralisation of international financial institutions with substantial devolution of authority and initiative to their regional and country offices (in an effort to increase their cultural, social and political sensitivity), but on the other hand, also have to do with the following (in no particular order and not exhaustively);
- Insisting on (longer) programme aid as opposed to (shorter) project aid;
- Calling for more recipient-driven aid as opposed to donor-centered packages of export earnings;
- A greater shared control of loans/grants by donor and recipient with an added role for NGOs in the partnership (the same as NGOs do watching over UN bodies and over global conferences;
- Policy measures that address the factors leading to the need for credits/loans;
- Setting up realistic frameworks which provide economic space for the poor to move out of poverty and that provide incentives for environmentally responsible economic behaviour.

27

Information Technology Outsourcing Goes Global

Many information technology jobs have been shifted to lower-cost countries, and may soon migrate onwards to regions offering even cheaper labour by affecting US job market. A recent study from the US analysts, Forrester Research gives some credence to this concern. The study suggests that as many as 3.3 million white-collar jobs, representing US $ 136 billion in wages, could shift from the US to lower-cost-countries by 2015. Some companies embracing so-called offshore outsourcing believe they can get better quality work at half the cost. It is a similar story in the United Kingdom, where the telecomes union, CWU, has strongly criticised British Telecom (BT) for plans, announced in March, to transfer 2,700 UK jobs to India this year. The jobs identified include directory enquiries, billing video conferencing and some telemarketing, CWU claims all BT divisions are exploring the possibility of transferring work to India and that thousands more jobs could be involved.

In its attack on BT, the CWU made it clear that it has no issue with India or with Indian workers. Its main argument is that, as a company which derives the bulk of its profits from UK customers, BT should have an obligations to support the British economy by employing local workers. The union also warns that, by moving jobs to India. BTG would be setting a very dangerous trend, which could see hundreds of thousands of British jobs potentially at risk.

How New a Trend

The transfer of data processing and data inputing from developed to developing countries dates back to the 1970s. Then, Caribbean islands such as Jamaica and Barbados led the development of "offshore" working. Initially, work typically consisted of routine administrative work, such as processing airline ticket stubs and credit card applications. Since then, however, much has changed; a sign perhaps of the apparent rise of the knowledge economy even in less developed countries.

India, in particular, has developed rapidly in recent years as a destination for software programming and IT-related work. Compound annual growth of more than 50 per cent had pushed the industry from a value of about US $ 175 million in 1989-90 to some US $ 5.7 billion ten years later. The Indian trade association, NASSCOM (National Association of Software and Service Companies), predicts the sector's turnover could reach US $ 85 billion by 2008.

NASSCOM has identified "IT-enabled" services as the focus for major expansion in the coming years. Such services include IT management (for example, network management and maintenance), payroll processing financial services and client management, including order processing and call centre operations. In practice, the last of these—call centre operations—has so far been the most important part of India's rapidly growing IT service market.

Call centres employ some 100.000 mostly young people in India. They are highly educated, usually holding degrees in engineering or computer science, and their working conditions are good—typically purpose-built blocks in IT parks outside cities such as Bangalore and Mumbai (Bombay). Call centre workers are trained to be effective when talking to customers abroad, so that staff dealing with the United States will be tutored to speak with a US accent and to understand US culture. Those handling calls from Britian are similarly trained on aspects of British culture, including the British weather. In some instances, staff are encouraged to take on

US or British names when talking to clients abroad, rather than using their own.

The main attraction of offshore outsourcing is the lower costs. Even though relatively well-paid by Indian standards, personnel costs are a fraction of Western wages. One British press report in 2001 suggested that Indian call centre workers earned the equivalent of $ 3,800 compared with UK workers' starting salaries of $ 19,000. More recently, the CEO of an Indian call centre company estimated that, in total, costs could be reduced by 40 to 60 per cent by moving to India.

Such developments are not limited to the English-speaking world. French companies are looking to African francophone countries, such as Mauritius and Morocco, as suitable destinations for call centres. Latin America provides an obvious location for Spanish companies looking to more offshore, while even German-language call centres have been established in lower-cost locations in developing countries.

This trend resembles the global relocation of work which took place a generation ago in the manufacturing sector. What is new is not simply that this trend is now being extended into the service sector, but also that middle-class and professional workers in developed countries are for the first time becoming directly affected. White-collar as well as blue-collar jobs are potentially migrating.

Trade unions in developed countries understandably cite the dangers of "social dumping" and a "race to the bottom". On the other hand, the development of indigenous software sectors in countries such as India does offer work opportunities for well-educated people to find work at home, as an alternative to seeking out work in North America or Europe—a practice sometimes derogatorily known as "body shopping".

North to South, or South to North

But the migration of jobs from North to South is only half of the picture. The other is South to North migration of workers (a familiar feature in the IT sector, at least up until the bursting of the dot.com bubble). Naturally enough, developing countries which have invested in educating young people are becoming increasingly concerned that such education is being used to seek work abroad.

Still, there is real concern among the unions that established levels of social protection and labour standards could be lost when jobs migrate to lower-cost regions of the world. Perhaps paradoxically, the Indian IT sector itself may have grounds to fear the same thing. The issue is that other countries are prepared to compete to provide ever-cheaper locations for work. A recent report on global outsourcing explored the potential of destinations such as Malaysia, Thailand, Vietnam, Mexico and Brazil, as well as Eastern European countries with established high-technology sectors, such as the Russian Federation, Ukraine and Bulgaria. It is however, China which is seen as the most likely next big player.

One trade union response to the fear of social dumping is to reassert their demand for the inclusion of core labour standards in future trade agreements negotiated through the World Trade Organisation. But there is another response happening at both ends of the outsourcing chain. This is the development of moves by unions to organize previously unorganised workers.

In the United States, people have been trying to persuade professionals in what has traditionally been a highly individualistic work culture to consider bargaining collectively with employers. "For many contractors and permatemps (agency workers with long-term employment with a single company), the prospect of obtaining that elusive permanent job, combined with fear of that never happening if they rock the boat in any way, often outweighs any motivation to mobilize around key workplace issues. Yet, for many, that permanent job never appears. Meanwhile in India, fledgling IT Professionals forums are developing in the states of Karnataka (focused on the cities of Bangalore and Mysore) and Andhra Pradesh (focussed on the state capital of Hyderabad). First established in 2000, the Forums have chosen not to use the term "trade union", which they claim has negative connotations among their target membership. However, the organisations have affiliated to the global union federation, Union Network International (UNI) Forum members say that, by working together collectively, they can better guard against professional risks and advance their careers. The forums mission statement is to become "the voice of IT professionals, to enrich and empower their knowledge, to promote their interests, and to contribute to the overall growth of the ICT (information and communications technologies) sector."

Enriching individuals knowledge may ultimately be one of the best protection measures against the risks of job migration, whether the flow is from the West towards India or from India towards other countries such as China. As with manufacturing a generation ago, the low-skilled, low value-added jobs will tend to be most mobile in a globalised world economy.

28

Markets Thrive on Information

Despite decades of structural adjustment pitched at freeing markets and years of policy emphasis on enabling small business, very many developing countries have suffered stagnating real incomes. Economic inertia is inevitable in any nation lacking functional business media. Journalists not only serve as public watchdogs in politics—they are also relevant for market efficiency.

In Ghana, five people died in riots triggered by the introduction of a value added tax in 1995. Imposed at the same rate and on the same products as the sales tax it was to replace, it was not a change that would morally have led to fighting in the streets. But journalists had got it wrong. According to their reports the tax would have drastically increased prices for consumers. In a country weary of painful structural adjustment policies, that was enough to trigger violence. But it wasn't true—the truth was that the journalists didn't understand the new tax. They had bought a line from interest groups that stood to lose out when the tax anomalies it was targeting were ended. Nonetheless, with the public at boiling point, the tax was abandoned.

This case was just one example of event caused by the lack of business journalism skills common to many emerging economies. It perfectly illustrates just how powerful business journalism can be. This event and many more like it prompted the World Bank, in 2002, to start training business journalists.

A Bridge for Public Understanding

While the watchdog role of political journalism is generally well understood, the similar role of business media has received very little attention in developing nations. Much emphasis has been placed on making financial decisions and transactions transparent. But that only helps to close down possibilities for graft, favour and simple incompetence when misbehaviour is made visible. Someone has to be watching, where data is produced that is read and understood by only a small circle of experts, transparency becomes at best accountability to powerful economic agents. There needs to be a bridge for public understanding.

A perfect example of this is currently unfolding in South Africa, where so called black economic empowerment (BEE) is driving a redistribution of wealth. Business media strongly support this politically correct trend. However, there are signs that the process is going seriously awry. This issue has been identified and even highlighted with data-rich press releases by financial experts. Nonetheless, the media have mostly ignored such information.

Last year, BEE drove a surge in merger and acquisition activity to a deal value of Rand 42.2bn. The business media reported this surge in strongly positive terms. Yet the data that gave this headline growth figure also highlighted that the majority of all of the country's BEE M&A deals were moving formerly white resources into the ownership of the black political elite: 60 per cent of the deals made in 2003 accrued to the companies of just two black politicians—Patrice Motsepe and Tokyo Sexwale.

This asset building by two men is far removed from the stated aims and ideals of black empowerment. Rather, it resembles the perversion of privatisation seen in almost all emerging economies from Russia outwards. Yet the business media in South Africa, instead of clamouring over such data, is close to silent. Reports are not even communicating the data neutrally, in order that readers can make their own judgements on whether this represents black empowerment.

Such situations show that transparency rules are of little use, unless active media are serving as watchdogs to alert the wider public. Distortions continue to occur under conditions of transparency unless they are reported. This, however, in not the worst damage resulting from poor media coverage.

Business media output, and the numbers of business journalists required to produce it, has burgeoned everywhere in the last two decades. A challenge exists across all nations in finding and retaining capable staff. They need to accept relatively moderate pay in spite of having the business and financial competence in huge demand throughout commerce.

The skills gap is far greater in development economies than in North America, western Europe or Japan. Business journalism entrants everywhere tend to be unfamiliar with the basic tenets of accounting, the financial markets, and economic relationships. But these skills are rarely present at any level of the profession in emerging economies. This results in business coverage primarily relaying headline growth figures with little explanation. It skirts detail, makes errors and is open to manipulation. Moreover, it fails to perform a series of functions vital to economic expansion and success.

Easily accessible business data tend to drive down consumer prices and to promote greater efficiency in processing and marketing. Competent media coverage contributes to making good strategic business decisions and helps to prevent business failures. All this adds up to more jobs and higher job security.

The Value of Comparative Data

In Kenya, in 1996, a group of journalists spent a collective 30 hours compiling a league table of interest rates on offer to Kenyan borrowers. Until then, the banks' loan rates and conditions had never been compiled and published. That is why the spread ran from 13 per cent to more than 30 per cent. Without information and comparison, there was no need for banks to compete on price. Kenyan borrowers took put luck-normally opting for the bank recommended by a relative or neighbour or coincidentally close to an oft-used thoroughfare. That was fine for anyone who stumbled across a 13 per cent loan. But for the very many who were paying 25 to 33 per cent it meant disaster. Such interest payments are tough on business anywhere. An initial lack of information in an uncompetitive market can easily doom projects to failure.

This lack of competition, rooted in an inefficient information market, has severely hampered Kenya's small and medium scale enterprise (SMEs). Nonetheless, the business media did not start to publish comparative interest rate offering on a continuous basis. Only years later, did the central bank step in with a regular information feed on loan interest rates which is now covered by the business press. In most rich countries, media companies would not have waited for such an official but would have gone on to research and publish comparative data.

This kind of information is often peripheral for large businesses, which have specialists dedicated to information collection and decision-making. Giant corporations employ lawyers, marketing managers, technical experts and other professionals. They also spend liberally in the fee-paying business information market, from market research reports to consultancy services. Small companies cannot afford such an effort for scanning their business environment. Yet the success of small business is a precondition of an economy's take-off.

In this US, small business produce more than half of the nation's total output. They also employ the majority of workers and create almost all of the country's net new jobs. In Europe, the picture is similar, with a third of the western European labour force in firms with less than 10 employees, excluding farms. Nothing can compensate for the economic gap created by a dormant or underperforming SME sector. But to achieve small business vibrancy, two hurdles must be overcome. Very many new businesses must be started, a significant proportion of which must succeed. In both areas, the business media plays a key role.

Support for Small Enterprises

To start new business, the economically active must understand entrepreneurship as a real and achievable option. People start business and it works. In the US a large slice of the business media is preoccupied with the realities of small business, carrying case studies and tales and experience. Consequently, running a small business is understood as an ever-present possibility.

Once small business emerges as a real option, the business media becomes essential in fuelling business expansion by signaling threats and highlighting opportunities. In the UK, where there are 10,000 business magazines and journals generating estimated annual revenues of more than 3.3bn, two-thirds of business people surveyed by the Periodical Publishers Association classified business magazines as essential reading. Across every sector and sub-sector, these publications serve to set up clubs and information networks, relaying market trends, technological data, job advertisements and information about competitors.

Marking business decisions without this kind of information represents a considerable handicap. In the UK, the Agridata Snapshot Readership Survey in 2002 found that 95 per cent of farmers read at least one farming publication. The majority of these same farmers also have internet connection, and can access relevant information directly. The idea of a majority of Ghanian farmers being internet connected and picking up US agricultural data, or information on the current Brazilian coffee harvest, and thus current coffee price trends, is close to absurd. It would, however, improve their business outlook. Entirely more viable is a single, capable agricultural publication to digest information relevant to farming in Ghana. Typically the business press should signal conferences, trade fair opportunities, buyers and sellers requirements, and, arriving at a low cover price, than pass on the information to a chain of many readers.

Similarly, radio in emerging markets has a reach and a capacity hardly ever deployed to relay relevant business news. Few journalists currently understand the importance of cash-flow. Yet between two-thirds and 90 per cent of new businesses fail because of cash-flow problems. This is surely reason enough to classify cash-flow management as a subject that deserves high attention even at the level of community radio.

More generally, it is hard to see how any industry without a forum used by all to advertise job vacancies can efficiently recruit appropriate personnel. Similarly, without a functioning business press, sliced around target audiences, small businesses are left with few ways of telling would-be customers that they exist. A flower producer cannot, with the single act of placing a cheap advertisement in the right business media, automatically reach flower buyers; an ingredients maker cannot affordably identify and reach a large line-up of food processors; a basketweaver cannot opt for a home improvement audience or the home improvement retail industry.

This loads market opportunities towards large, established, normally multi-national players. They can afford to spend heavily on advertising using billboards, national newspapers and broadcast media. African farmers might be able to source equipment locally, if they knew it was available. Instead the only equipment they know of is that which is backed by big marketing spends.

In the absence of a competent business press, the SME engine of economic growth remains hamstrung. Yet while the link between a competent mainstream media and democracy is accepted as a tenet of the current orthodoxy, there is in such understanding of the relationship between the business media and economic success.

29

Consumption Bomb

It is three decades since we passed the peak world population growth rate of 2.04 per cent. Annual additions too are now a decade past their peak of 86 million a year. They are currently running at 78 million a year and are heading downwards. A peak in total numbers, however, still lies at least four or five decades ahead. On the UN Population Division's 1998 projections, the total is likely to reach 8.9 billion in 2050. The long range medium projection, which has not been updated since 1996, expects world population to level out at just under 11 billion in 2200 AD.

However, this is based on assumptions that are increasingly questionable. More and more countries are reaching levels of female fertility that are not enough for replacement—below 2.1 children over the lifetime of each women. At the latest count there are 61 countries in this category. Of this 23 had very low fertility, below 1.5.

The situation is unprecedented in times of global peace on economic growth. The UN medium projection assumes that where fertility is very low it will rise again to 1.7-1.9 children per woman. In all countries where fertility is currently above replacement level of 2.1, it assumes that it will not fall below that level.

Yet fertility has fallen below replacement level in so many countries, which such different cultures and different stages of economic growth, that is increasingly looking as if low fertility may be here to stay. If this became the case, then world population may peak at some where between 8 and 9 billion. Thereafter it may well begin to decline. The 1996 long range low projection has world population falling to 5.6 billion in 2100 AD.

None of this means that reproductive rights should have lower priority in future. Their contribution to the health and welfare of women and children are clear. Many poor countries in Africa and South Asia face huge population increases which will be hard to accommodate without major problems of land and water scarcity. In these areas reproductive rights receive a very high priority.

Increasingly our concern must focus on consumption, and how we can cope with the effects of its inexorable increase. Over the past 25 years world population increased by 53 per cent, but world consumption per person (Measured by income) by only 39 per cent. Assume that consumption per person will rise 100 per cent, while population will rise by only half that amount. As time goes on the preponderance of consumption will increase more and more.

There is a crucial difference between population and consumption aspirations. If fully assured of children's survival most people have quite modest desire for family size. But their desire to consume knows no upper bounds. As wealth increases, people double-up their possessions; two or three cars, two bathrooms, two rooms with all contents, two or three holidays a year.

Appliances improve every year and old ones "need" replacing. New needs are created that never existed before. Globalisation is making products cheaper than ever. TVs are no longer uncommon even in African shanty towns. The number of households is increasing as people live longer and family breakdown becomes more common. Smaller households consume considerably more per cent than large. Moreover, consumption is politically very difficult to restrain. No one can get elected promising people they can earn and spend less, or re-elected if they fulfil their promises.

In view of this much of the burden of reducing our environmental impact will rest on technology. Technology will have to deliver major shifts in improving resource productivity, and in reducing the amount of waste we create. All our institutions and forms of management which affect technology will need to be geared to this end.

In some areas the record has been good and looks likely to remain so. Productivity has kept up with demand in the case of resources that are traded on markets, and that are under the direct control of people or companies affected by shortages or prices. Global food production has kept pace with demand: although land and cereal production per person has declined, average intakes of calories and protein have continued to improve and are at record levels. Malnutrition persists, but this is due to poverty and landlessness, not to the inability of the world to produce enough food. We have not encountered any limiting shortage of any key mineral resources or of energy. Nor are we likely to, because we continually economise and find substitutes, there has been a gradual reduction in the material used for each unit of production.

The prospects are much worse for resources that are not traded on markets or subject to sustainable management, as yet. These include groundwater, state forests, ocean fish, bio-diversity in general. They include communal waste sinks like rivers, lakes and oceans, and the global atmosphere. In all of these areas it looks likely that things will get quite a lot worse before they get better.

These kinds of resources and sinks are not under the direct control of people affected by shortage or damage. People wishing to change the way a common resource or sink is used or managed have to pass through the legal or political system. They must organise, take out lawsuits against polluters, pressurise legislators and so on. Political responses are typically slow. Usually the majority of voters have to be convinced of the need for action before politicians will risk taking action. Even then powerful and rich vested interest will lobby hard for the status quo, and will often succeed in frustrating changes that are desired by a global majority. America's coal, oil, and car lobbies have stood in the way of any significant US commitment to reduce carbon-di-oxide output, and the US is the world's largest emitter of carbon-di-oxide.

Usually there has to be very widespread and very visible environmental damage before action is taken. The thinning of the ozone layer fitted that category well and the response was swift. North Atlantic fishing reached that point in the 1990s, yet politicians shied away from taking adequate action until the last moment: fishing stocks plummeted and there was massive job loss. Global warming is still long way from the damage being widespread enough, and attributable clearly enough to human activities, for politicians to be ready to speed up the move into renewable energy.

The question with the common resources and sinks is always: will we react in time? The answer is all the more difficult because we usually don't know in advance what is "in time." Many critical changes are subject to threshold effects. When a certain point is crossed, very sudden and disastrous change can occur with little warning. In many cases we do not know where the thresholds lie.

Prudence dictates a preventive approach—a stitch in time saves nine. But the history of environmental problems shows that politicians rarely act decisively until the brink is reached, and it will always be touch and go whether we are pushed over it or not.

30

The Dematerialisation of the World Economy

The first Industrial Revolution marked the transition from robber-and-plunder colonialism to the systematic development of the "overseas" territories in the framework of an international division of labour between raw material suppliers and manufacturers of finished goods. There was an "historic integration" of the colonised areas in the development of their parent-states. What will the third Industrial Revolution do for the Third World ? Will it now come to an "historic separation" ?

The end of the East-West conflict was reason enough to talk about a radical change in world politics. But at the same time an upheaval in the world economy is taking place that possibly will have even wider impacts. As a reference point for the following thoughts, three dimensions of this change are pointed out:

1. the upgrading of processing information rather than materials as object of economic activity (technological dimension);

2. the evolvement of global communications networks (socio-cultural dimension);

3. the change of the nature of work (socio-economic dimension).

All three dimensions can be summarised under the buzzphrase "tertialisation of the world economy."

In that respect, talk of the "Third Industrial Revolution" is misleading. It is not about a third epoch of industrialisation, but about the beginning of a de-industrialisation, the transition from the industrial to the information society.

Historic Separation?

In the 1960s and early 1970s, there was often talk of the Third World as the Third Sector of the world economy. Also then the Third World was not much more than an "imaginary community". But as such it had a certain significance in world politics. This implied not only its strategic role in the East-West conflict and its ideological function as the supporter of different "third paths" between capitalism and socialism. It was also about the Third World's attested "chaos power". That linked the fear (in the North) and the hope (in the South) that the developing countries would be in a position to cut off the industrial nations from supplies of important raw materials, thus putting them under pressure. But it was soon seen that both sides had over estimated this possibility, even with regard to oil. Instead of supply bottlenecks arising, raw materials prices plummeted. For some commodities, the fall in prices exceeded those of the Great Depression of 1929/30.

This was due, inter alia, to the conjunction of lower demand from the industrial nations and expansion of production by the raw materials suppliers. Business activities dependent upon the supply of raw materials are tending to lose importance compared with the overall development of the global economy. The reason for this is to be seen in the transition from a material to an information economy.

This transition is taking place in line with the revolutionising of data transmission and the expansion of financial transactions which are not directly related to changes in the production of materials. The speed of the changes is remarkable.

However, the dematerialisation of business activities does not lead to decoupling of the Third World from the world economy. Declining market shares in world trade are not the expression of separation, but a loss of the affected countries positions in the world economy. Thus, the impact of dematerialisation is "only" that the negotiating positions of raw materials suppliers vis–a–vis the industrial nations will deteriorate further.

Differentiation of the Third World

But the radical change in the global economy is affecting some developing countries worse than others. Sub–saharan Africa and some countries in West and South Asia and Latin America are being pushed back further. The oil–producing countries with their high per capita export earnings will be able to hold their positions in the world economy for some time to come. The threshold countries of East and South-East Asia can expand theirs so long as they can continue to attract a growing share of global industrial production, and at the same time participate in the tertialisation of the world economy in the shape of rapidly-growing financial transactions. Thereby it should be noted that the degree of tertialisation in itself is not an adequate indicator for economic avant-gardism. Brazil exhibits a high degree of tertialisation in combination with a low macro-economic development dynamics. A good part of its tertialisation is being achieved by speculative financial transactions with their inherently greater risks and uncertainties than in the industrial countries. Such dangers have been demonstrated by Mexico's peso crisis and its repercussions on the whole of Latin America.

In some Third World countries, a "location annuity" has replaced the old raw materials one. Here it's about providing locations for off-shore transactions which offer international capital traders a maximum of freedom of movement combined with low taxation. Suitable for such operations are small countries which, despite low levy rates, achieve significant income in macro-economic terms.

The radical changes in the world economy are spurring the differentiation of the Third World without, however, necessarily fostering a dissolution of the Third World as an "imaginary community". It is precisely the advanced countries of East and South-East Asia that are showing a certain interest in the formulation of joint positions of the "South" in order to secure their own positional gains in the global economy. It's not by chance that the non-aligned countries and the Group of 77 have formed a joint coordination committee, and that the ASEAN countries are changing course on the international human rights policy.

Hitherto, the developing countries' strategy was to broaden the concept of human rights as a justification for demands on the industrial nations. But of late some developing countries, led by the ASEAN states, have questioned the universal validity of human rights even after their universality was confirmed by consensus at the Conference on Human Rights in Vienna in 1993. Playing a role in this policy is the governments' fear that due to the expansion of global communications networks, the behaviour patterns and preferences of their own people could in some way become similar to those of the West. As the rulers see it, that would be detrimental to the continuation of the development models practised so far.

Internet Creates New Cultural Dimension

Much information which Asian governments view as subversive in already globally available on the internet. The old struggle over the world information order, which at first was primarily a clinch between East and West, is thus taking on a new dimension. For with the growing importance of computer literacy to a country's ability to assert itself on world markets, the Asian threshold countries have not only an interest in controlling the on-line communication but also to expand it and the know-how that it requires.

Even the critics of any interventions in the internet and other global communication networks must admit that modern communication technologies are politically blind and their use in itself does not represent progress. The setting up and expansion of global information highways will offer forum not only to people who want to use it for education and enlightenment, but also to all shades of fundamentalists. These highways will not necessarily bring the misery of many Third World regions closer to the industrial countries, but possibly rather strengthen the tendency to process all world events as entertainment.

Global Two-thirds Society

The gravest aspect of the current upheaval in the world economy is its negative impact on jobs. The information economy needs for fewer workers than an economy based on materials. Instead, the demands on the skills of the workers are growing. Twenty per cent of the world workforce will in future be employed as (overworked) "intelligence workers". Eighty per cent will work part-time, if they are not underemployed or jobless. So the tertialisation of the global economy delivers more underemployment rather than more leisure time. The workers who are rationalised out of their jobs in the industrial sector cannot be absorbed by the service sector because it, too, is not left untouched by rationalisation measures. The civil service is also cutting back on staff. At all levels, there's a race to make the greatest possible savings on payrolls. At the same time, there's growing pressure to cut costs in providing for the victims of this development. That means thinning out the social security safety net.

The bottom line is that the two-thirds society, which developmental action groups hitherto assumed was limited to the Third World, is spreading worldwide. That, however, will not in the foreseeable future lead to an amendment of the North-South disparities. It's true that the change in the global economy is taking place faster, and to a greater extent in the industrial nations. But rationalisation is also happening in the developing countries in a bid to boost their competitiveness. So the upheaval in the world economy aggravates the problems which exist in a majority of the developing countries, while creating new ones in the industrial nations. The need for action on the North-South policy is growing, among the industrial nations. The need for action on the North-South Policy is growing, while the industrial nations' scope for concessions and compromises is shrinking. The new social question which is now crystallizing at global level is not being answered. The consequences are unforeseeable.

Another Loser?

It's more probable that a sharpening of the North--South confrontation is to be reckoned with. For the industrial nations will attempt to keep the social costs of the information economy at bay for as long as possible. The trade unions will thereby compete with the developing countries for jobs for their members. But this policy has its limits precisely because of the peaking of the problems in the industrial nations. Overstepping these limits means war and passively accepting them chaos and social decay. Solutions could be sought in two directions: effective taxation of the information economies and the creation of jobs in the non-profit sector. But it's possible there are no global solutions for global problems. That would mean for at least part of the Third World a renewal of the old debate on partial decoupling from the world economy.

31

Crisis and New Orientation of Development Policy

The poverty in the South, the dislocations in the East, and the orientation crisis in the North are not isolated phenomena. Rather, they represent an alarming amalgamation of dangers that are globally interlinked.

The low effectiveness of international economic and development policy is rooted in two outdated paradigms on which the present worldwide strategy of economic development is based, namely that:

1. The Western social and economic model optimizes the activation of productive forces—independent of the development stage of a country and its culture and therefore is best suited to satisfy basic needs;

2. It is possible to launch the development of a society from the outside within a few decades—without regard to is cultural and historical background—through external input of money, goods, technology, expertise, and personnel.

The twin paradigms of the timelessness and transferability combined with cultural ecological, and financial restrictions—have led international cooperation and development down the wrong path.

Only if we acknowledge the true dimensions of the global dangers, if we recognize the limitations and shortcomings of existing political instruments, and identify outdated theories and contradictory special interests, can we outline the cornerstones of a new policy of global cooperation.

Cornerstones of a New Development Policy

Starting with critical review of the shortcomings and paradigms of the prevailing development strategy, the following ten cornerstones of a new development policy are offered for discussion:

1. *Broaden the Concept of Development*

Whether a society is considered developed depends on the size of its per-capita Gross National Product (GNP). Accordingly, the world is divided into a developed, semi developed, and underdeveloped world. The yardstick for development, which has become the norm in the industrial countries, is one-dimensional: It only measures the monetary value of goods and services that are exchanged in the marketplace. This standard is too narrow economically because it compresses the multitude and complexity of cultural, societal, historical. social,. and human values into a single economic category.

At the most, there can and should be agreement on what development and progress should not bring about: Inability to find enough work to meet the most basic needs; exploitation and oppression of people; loss of cultural wealth and institutions; destruction of natural resources. These, however, are the very values that are sacrificed by the prevailing development strategy. In the future, development policy must do all it can to stop the loss of skills and self-reliance, the plunder of natural resources, the erosion of cultural values, the violation of human dignity and human rights. Initiatives must prevail which are orientated on these values, and not just on the GNP.

2. *Concentrate Development Strategy on the Internal Potential of Developing Countries*

There must be an end to the manic fixation of

development strategy on external inputs and external markets. A new development policy must, above all, improve internal conditions for a productive economy, promote domestic production factors on a broad basis, protect cultural and natural resources, and greatly increase the domestic supply of basic goods. Wherever external inputs are unavoidable, credits must be strictly tied to the productivity and the ability of a country to absorb transfers. External transfers should be concentrated on "Software" for health, education, social participation administative, and legal jurisdiction. Such an approach could also promote training and indigenous technologies, which are so important for economic development.

The set-up and expansion of the productive sectors must be decided, planned, and implemented by the developing countries themselves, and they must assume full responsibility. The external pressures, which force the developing countries into full integration with the world market, must be removed. This presupposes a structural reduction of interest rates.

3. *Make Development Policy a Central Feature of Politics*

Development policy must take the lead in mobilizing the various political forces and government departments to join the fight against the growing global dangers. It must ensure that the actions of all political departments are compatible with development policy is possible only if it becomes the central task of all political sectors, comparable to social and environmental policies, and the central goal of all policies. If development policy is to become a central task, development problems must become a priority in parliament and government. Society must understand that it is in the national interest to accept great global responsibilities.

4. *Reform the World Economy*

The industrial countries must abolish their protectionism in agriculture 'as well the processed goods sector. Simultaneously, the developing countries need to be protected selectively and for a limited time against imports from the industrial countries. The undifferentiated structural adjustment policies imposed by the IMF must be revised. The trend toward regionalisation of the world economy should not be opposed; rather, in the interest of both South and East, it must be regulated constructively to form a new, regionally based world trade structure.

A reform of the international finance system is urgently needed: Interest and exchange rates should not "mirror the national interests of the big industrial states and the special interests of large banks and venture capital. Rather, they must reflect the global interest in monetary stability lower and stable interest rates, and sufficient development financing.

However, strengthening the international financial institutions is in the global interest only if the countries of the southern and eastern hemispheres are allowed to exert some influence. An international financial court must guarantee that violations of strict regulations to ensure international stability and solvency can be protested in a court of law.

5. *Redesign the Industrial Society*

As a global social and environmental policy, the new development policy must induce the industrial countries to give up their excessive consumption of air, water, soil, resources, and space. Increased utilisation of energy-conservation measures and environmentally friendly technologies is overdue. The economic and social policies of the industrial nations must promote balance rather than growth. This requires radical changes in traditional economic thinking, habits, structures and processes.

In view of limited world resources, unsatisfied existential needs in South and East, and continuous population growth in the South, the only premise for the future can be: Growth rates in the South must be higher than in the North, but they should no longer be in the North, but they should no longer be induced primarily by growth in the North. If economic policies continue to call for the North to provide the locomotive, the North will have to continue to acquire more resources than the South.

The North must relinquish 'the remaining growth frontiers to the South and East. The South must use this opportunity to activate its internal dynamic potential rather than integrate its economy with the North. However, ecological and social controls must be established at a much earlier stage than was the case in Europe.

6. *Strengthen Development Cooperation*

The share of official development assistance as a percentage of GNP, which dropped from 0.48 per cent in 1982 to 0.34 per cent in 1995 must be gradually raised again and reach at least 0.7 per cent in the year 2000—a goal which OECD established as early as two decades ago and which was reconfirmed at the Rio Earth Summit.

However, we must not succumb to the illusion that a doubling of ODA funds will even remotely meet the financial needs of South and East. State development policy must use its scarce public funds more effectively in the future. It must use restraint whenever partners in the developing countries can accomplish a task on their own and private initiatives and private enterprise are more competent to do the job. The government should be directly engaged only when it can be relatively more productive. Otherwise, it should limit itself to subsidizing private organisations.

7. *New Orientation for Development Cooperation*

The state and its implementation agencies must abandon all direct responsibility for any projects which require unbureaucratic action, economic efficiency, and long term productivity. It must make a much greater effort to involve NGO's and private venture capital in development projects. At the same time, the state must insist and guarantee that private actions are compatible with social and ecological concerns.

In the future, the main thrust of government projects should be the promotion of the internal potential of a country. This comprises the political and administrative framework conditions of a humane, socially and ecologically sound development: Constitutional government, social institutions which facilitate broad participation of the population in politics, society, and economy; efficient savings, credit, fiscal and financial systems; mechanisms for income, property, and land distribution which promote productivity, justice, and social peace. In addition of this "software" of development, the following is needed: A regimen for the protection of resources and environment; measures to prevent the short term sellout of natural resources; elementary and general education and training, health care and social safety nets; capacities to develop science and technology.

8. *Reduce the Debt Service and Activate Private Capital*

Public funds must be used to a greater degree for the financial rehabilitation of highly indebted countries in South and East; external demands for interest and principal payments must be adapted to the economic capacity of the respective country and its ability to execute external capital transfers.

Within the framework of international insolvency regulations, initiatives must be developed as a condition for the continuance of the present rules for write-offs—which ensure effective cooperation from the banks and alleviate the heavy burden of private credits, with their high interest rates.

State development policy and private business interests should supplement each other. Government promotion of private enterprise initiatives for exports, investment, and employment in the developing countries must take into account their compatibility with development. In reverse, private engagements which effectively promote development must be actively supported by the government. A separate line item must be established in the development budget for such activation of private capital.

9. *Set Regional Priorities*

State development cooperation has been scattering its scarce funds not only among too many sectors, but also among too many partners. In the future, public funds must be concentrated regionally. More emphasis must be placed on regional programmes, and development cooperation with threshold countries must be enhanced. A portion of public funds should be set aside to provide an incentive for threshold countries to assist the poorer nations in their own region as well as deal with poverty in their own country.

The new development policy could then also help lessen ethnic-national conflicts and promote peace by sponsoring regional cooperation in joint development projects. For this purpose, regional development funds must be set up for cooperation in the transportation, energy, trade, and finance sectors and last, but not least for regional security systems and disarmament. Such regional funds could also provide the means to project refugees and improve their prospects for an eventual return to their homelands.

Bibliography

Ackoff, R.L., *Redesigning the Future: A Systems Approach to Societal Problems* (John Wiley, 1974).

Adelman, I., et al. *Economic Growth and Social Equality in Developing Countries* (California, Standford University, 1967).

Aggarwal, Y.P., *Education and Human Resource Development* (New Delhi, Commonwealth, 1988).

Amirk Singh., 'New Policy on Education: Two Years Later', *Economic and Political Weekly*, Special Number, Vol. XXIII, Nos. 45, 46 & 47, pp. 2479-92.

Anand, Mulk Raj, 'A Nation of Illiterates' *The Tribune*. Feb. 12, 1991.

Anderson, C.A., 'A Skeptical Note on Education and Mobility, A.H. Halsey, & Others (ed)—*Education Economy and Society*, (New York, The Free Press, 1969), pp. 164-182.

Anderson, C.A., 'Access to Higher Education and Economic Development' in *Halsey, A.H. (Ed) Op. cit.* Work. pp. 252-268.

Anderson, C.A. and Bowman, M.J., *Education and Economic Development* (Chicago, 1965).

Anon, *'The Pressure of Economic Change'* in *A.H. Halsey, (Ed), op. cit.* pp. 22-30.

Anon, 'All-out Bid to Tap Human Resources', *The Economic Times* (Supplement), Dec. 20, 1984, pp. 1-3.

Asharaya, P., 'Education: Politics and Social Structure', *Economic & Political Weekly*, Vol. XX, No. 42, Oct. 19, 1985, pp. 1785-89.

Bantock, G.A. *Education and Values*, (London, Faber & Faber, 1966).

Bauer, R.A. (Ed), *Social Indicators* (Cambridge and London, MIT Press, 1966).

Becker, Garry S., *Human Capital* (Princeton, Princeton University Press, 1964).

Becker, Garry S., *Human Capital: A Theoretical and Empirical Analysis with Special Reference to Education,* (New York, NBER, 1974).

Ben-Porath, Yoram. 'The Production of Human Capital and the Life Cycle of Earnings', *The Journal of Political Economy,* August, 1967, pp. 352-65.

Benson, Charles S. *Perspectives on the Economics of Education* (Boston, Houghton Mifflin Company, 1963).

Bhalla, G.S. and Bhalla, H.S. 'Human Resource Development for Rural Poor', Paper Presented at the U.G.C. *National Seminar,* Held at G.K. I.A.S. in Rural Development, Punjabi University, Campus, Damdama Sahib).

Bhatia, S.K., 'Challenges in Human Resource Management', *Indian Management,* Vol. 25, No. 8, August 1986, pp. 5-12.

Blaug, Mark (Ed), *Economics of Education-I* (New York, Penguin, 1968).

Blaug, Mark (Ed), *Economics of Education-II* (New York, Penguin, 1969).

Blaug, Mark, *An Introduction to the Economics of Education* (New York, Penguin, 1970).

Blaug, Mark, 'The Empirical Status of Human Capital Theory: Slightly Jaundiced Survey', *Journal of Economic Literature,* Vol. 14, No. 3, September 1976, pp. 827-55.

Boulding, K., *The Meaning of the Twentieth Century* (London, Allen & Unwin, 1965).

Bowman, M.J., 'Education and Economic Growth *in King, T.* (Ed), *Education and Income* (Staff Working Paper No. 402, Washington, World Bank, 1980) pp. 1-71.

Bowman, M.J., 'The Human Investment Revolution in Economic Thought', *Sociology of Education 39/2* (Spring), pp. 111-37.

Brown, Murraya (Ed), *The Theory and Empirical Analysis of Production* (New York, NBER, 1967).

Brownstein, L., *Education and Development in Rural Kenya* (New York, Praeger, 1972).

Burgess, T., et. al., *Manpower and Educational Development in India* (London, Oliver & Boynd).

Byars, L.L. and Rue, L.W., *Human Resource Management* (Illinois, Irwin Homewood).

Chattopadhyay, G., 'Education: The Authority to Learn or the Authority of the Bowl of Hemlock' in *Decision* (IIM, Calcutta), Vol. 16, No. 1, Jan-March, 1989, pp. 22-33.

Cheema, C.S. 'The Challenges of Human Resource Development in Rural Punjab'—Paper Presented 'at *U.G.C. National Seminar* Held at G.K. I.A.S. in Rural Development, Punjabi University Campus, Damdama Sahib).

Clark, Harold F., 'The Return on Educational Investment' in C.S. Benson, (Ed), *Op. cit.*, 1963, pp. 24-32.

Coombs, P.H. and Manzoor Ahmed, *Attacking Rural Poverty: Non-Formal Education Can Help* (John Hopkins University Press, 1974).

Coombs, P.H., *The World Crisis in Education: The View From Eighties* (Oxford, OUP, 1985).

Correa, Hector, *The Economics of Human Resources* (Amsterdam, North-Holland, 1963).

Curle, Adam, 'Some Aspects of Educational Planning in Underdeveloped Areas, *Harvard Educational Review*, Vol. 32, No. 3, 1962.

D' Souza, A.A. and De Souza., *A Population Growth and Human Development* (Delhi, ISI, 1974).

Datta, S., 'Human Resource Development',, *Man and* Development, Vol. 8, No. 1, March 1986, pp. 9-17.

Davis, R.G., *Planning Human Resource Development*, (Chicago, 1966).

Davis, Russel G. *Planning Human 'Resource Development: Education Models and Schemata* (Chicago, CSED, Harvard University, 1966).

Denison, Edward F., 'Education and Growth' in Benson, C.S. (Ed), *Op. cit.*, pp. 33-42.

Desai A.R. *Social Background* of *Indian Nationalism* (Bombay, Popular, 1966).

Deshmukh, C.D. 'Management and Administration: New Trends', *Training Abstracts 17,* New Delhi Training Division, 1972.

Dey, B., 'On Costing Education' in Pandit's *Measurement of Cost Productivity and Efficiency of Education* (New Delhi, NCERT, 1969), pp. 14-26.

Dey, B. 'Training in the Civil Services: Plea for A Holistic Construal', *Indian Journal of Public Administration* Vol. XXIV, No. 4, Oct.-Dec. 1982.,

Drucker, Peter F. 'The Educational Revolution' in Halsey and Others (Ed) *Op. cit.*, pp. 15-21.

Drucker, Peter, F., *Managing in Turbulent Times* (William Heinemann, 1980).

Dwivedi, R.S., *Management of Human Resources: A Behavioural Approach to Personnel* (New Delhi, Oxford & IBH, 1982).

Farooq, Khan A., 'Development of Human Resources', *The Economic Times,* September 22, 1984.

Gandhi, Rajiv, 'New National Policy on Education', *Inaugural Address* at the Conference of Education Ministers at New Delhi, August 29,1985.

Gill, K.S., 'Agricultural Development in Punjab' in Johar and Khanna's (Ed), *Studies in Punjab Economy* (Aniritsar, GNDU, 1983).

Gore, M.S., 'Literacy: Equaliser of Opportunity', *Democratic World,* March 31, 1991, Vol. XX, No. 13.

Gostkowski, Z. *Towards a System of Human Resources Indicators for Less-developed Countries'* (The Polish Academy of Sciences).

Government of India, *Challenges of Education: A Policy Perspective* (Government of India, Ministry of Education, 1985).

Government of India, *National Policy on Education* (New Delhi, Govt. of India, 1986).

Government of India, *National Policy on Education : Programme of Action* (New Delhi, Govt. of India, 1986).

Groves, Harold M., 'Education and Economic Growth' in C.S. Benson, (Ed), *Op. cit.*, pp. 7-11.

Halsey, A.H. and Others (Ed), *Education, Economy and Society* (New York, The Free Press, 1969).

Harbison, F., 'The Prime Movers of Innovations' in Halsey, A.H. & Others (Ed) *Op. cit.*

Harbison, F. *Human Resources as the Wealth of Nations* (London, OUP, 1973).

Harbison, F. and Myers, C.A. *Education, Manpower and Economic Growth* (New York, 1974).

Havighurst, R.J., 'Education and Social Mobility' in Four Societies' in A.H. Halsey, & Others (Ed), *Op. cit.*, pp. 105-120.

Heyneman, S.P., *Improving the Quality of Education in Developing Countries* (Washington, World Bank, 1983).

Heyneman, S.P. and White, D.S., *The Quality of Education and Economic Development* (Washington, World Bank, 1986).

Hicks, Norman, *Economic Growth and Human Resources,* World Bank, Staff Paper No. 408, (Washington, World Bank, 1980).

Hilton School of. *Human Resource Development* (Vellore, ISSR, 1989).

Huq, M. S., *Education, Manpower and Development in South and South-East Asia* (Delhi, Sterling, 1975).

Hussain, Majid, *Agricultural Geography* (New Delhi, Inter-India, 1986).

Jagannathan, N., 'Gender Equality in Education', *University News,* Vol. XXIX, No. 5, Feb. 4, 1991, pp. 1-5.

Jamison, D.T. and Laurence, J.L., *Farmer Education and Farm Efficiency* (Baltimore, John Hopkins, 1982).

Jhingan, M.L., *The Economics of Development and Planning* (New Delhi, Vikas, 1975).

Johnson, D. Gale., 'Economics and the Educational System, in C.S. Benson, (Ed), *Op. cit.*, pp. 374-80.

Joshi, P.C., 'Role of Culture in Social Transformation and National Integration, *Economic and Political Weekly,* Vol. XXI, No. 28.

Kamat, A.R., *Progress of Education in Rural Maharashtra* (Pune, Gokhale Institute of Politics and Economics, 1968).

Khanna, G., Parkash, S. and Bansal, R.K., *Unit Cost of College Education in Punjab* (Patiala, Punjabi University, 1985) Mimeo.

Khullar, K.K., 'Four Decades of Education', *Yojana*, Vol. 33, No. 8, Nov. 1-15,1989, pp. 12-4.

King, T. (Ed)., *Education and Income*, World Bank Staff Working, Paper No. 402 (Washington, World Bank, 1980).

Kirpal, P. 'How to Plan Education of the Future', *Yojana*, Vol. 33, No. 14 & 15, August, 1989.

Kothari, Commission, *Report of the Education Commission: 1964-66* (Delhi, Government of India, 1970).

Kothari, V.N. and Panchamukhi, P.R., 'Economics of Education: A Trend Report' in *ICSSR's A Survey of Research in Economics* (New Delhi, 1980), pp. 169-238.

Krishnamurthy, H.V. 'Human Resource Development Strategy For 21st Century; P.U. *Management Review*, Vol. 9, Nos. 1 & 2, Jan-Feb. 1986, pp. 79-89.

Kulkarni, V.G. 'Alternatives in Education' *Man & Development* (Vol. VIII), March 1985, pp. 25-58.

Lipton, *Why Poor Stay Poor: A Study of Urban Bias in World Development* (London, Templesmith, 1977).

MacNamara, R.S. *The Assualt on World Poverty* (Washington, World Bank, 1975).

Mahajan, V.S. 'Whither National Policy: Education', *The Tribune*, Feb. 24, 1991, p. 8.

Majumdar, Tapas. *Investment in Education and Social Choice*, (New York, Cambridge University Press, 1983).

Marshall, Alfred. 'Education and Invention' in Benson, C.S.(Ed), *Op. cit.*, pp. 82-83.

Mathur, B.L. (Ed)., *Human Resource Development: Strategic Approaches and Experiences*, (Jaipur, Arihant, 1989).

Mathur, R.N., *Population Analysis and Studies* (Allahabad, Chugh).

Megginson, L.C., *Personnel and Human Resource Administration,* 1974.

Mehta, M.M., *Human Resource Development Planning,* (Delhi, Macmillan, 1976).

Mingat, Alan and Tan, Jee-Pang. *Analytical Tools for Sector Work in Education* (Baltimore/London, John Hopkins University Press, 1988).

Mishra, L. 'Literacy: Now or Never' in *Yojana,* Vol. 34, No. 20, Nov. 1-15, 1990, pp. 4-5.

Misra, S.K. and Puri, V.K., *Development and Planning: Theory and Practice,* (Bombay, Himalaya, 1986).

Moddie, A.D. *Explorations in Management Development* (New Delhi, AIMA, 1976).

Myrdal, G., *Asian Drama* (Penguin, 1963).

Nadler, L., *Developing Human Resources* (Texas, Concepts, 1979).

Nadler, L., *The Handbook of Human Resources Development* (John Willey, 1984).

Nallagounden, A.M. 'Investment in Education in India' *Journal of Human Resource,* Vol. 2, No. 3, Summer-1967, pp. 347-58.

Nandedkar, V.G., 'Human Resource: Both An End and Means', Yojana, Vol. 34, Nos. 1 & 2, Jan. 26, 1990, pp. 50-53.

National Council of Educational Research and Training. *The Fourth All India Education Survey* (New Delhi, NCERT, 1982).

Niland, John R., *The Producation of Manpower Specialists: A Volume of Selected Papers* (New York, Cornell University, 1971).

Nurkse, R., *Problems of Capital Formation in Underdeveloped Countries,* (New Delhi, OUP, 1973).

OECD, *Education in OECD Developing Countries: Trends and Perspectives,* (France, OECD,, 1974).

Ota, Masao. 'Quantitative Method for the Planning of Human Resource Development', *Research Bulletin of the National Institute for Educational Reasearch,* No. 11, 1972, pp. 25-41.

Panchamukhi, V.R. Leading Issues in Human Resource Development in India' in P.R. Brahmananda, and V.R. Panchamukhi, (Ed), *Development Process of the Indian Economy, (Bombay,* Himalaya, 1987), pp. 1060-1108.

Pandit, H.N., *Measurement of Cost Productivity and Efficiency of Education* (Delhi, NCERT, 1969).

Rao, B.S., 'Developing Human Resources in Rural Areas: Some Basic Propositions' in 'M.K. Rao and P.P. Sharma, (Ed), *Human Resource Development for Rural Development* (Bombay, Himalaya, 1989), pp. 3-6.

Rao, N.K. and Sharma, P.P., *Human Resource Development for Rural Development* (Bombay, Himalaya, 1989).

Rao, T.V., 'Some Thoughts on HRD in Education', *Indian Journal of Training and Development* (July-Sept., 1986, pp. 135-7.

Rao, T.V., et al., *Alternative Approaches and Strategies of Human Resource Development* (Jaipur, Rawat, 1988).

Rao, T.V., 'Planning for Human Resources Development' in Mathur, B.L. (Ed.), *Op. cit.*

Rao, V.L., 'Human Element in Economic Development' in Rao, M.K. and Sharma, P.P. (Ed), *Op. cit.*, pp. 20-27.

Rao, V.K. R.V., *Education and Human Resource Development* (Bombay, Allied, 1960).

Ravishankar, S., et al., *Human Resource Development: In a Changing Environment* (Bombay, Dhruv & Deep, 1988).

Raza, Moonis, et al., *Education and the Future: An Indian Perspective,* A UNESCO Sponsored Study (New Delhi, NIEPA, 1983).

Raza, Moonis (Ed), *Educational Planning: A Long Term Perspective* (Delhi, Concept., 1986).

Ruark, Henry C. (jr.), 'Technology and Education' in *Benson,* C.S. (Ed), *Op. cit.*, pp. 381-92.

Sapra, C.L. and Aggarwal, Y. (Ed), *Education in India: Critical Issues* (New Delhi, National, 1987).

Saxena, J.P., et al., 'Human Resource Development Strategy', for India's Seventh Plan', *The Economic Times,* July 25, 1984.

Schelsky, H., 'Technical Change and Educational Consequences', in Halsey (Ed), *Op. cit.*, pp. 31-6.

Pandit, H.N. A Study in Unit Costs at School Stage in India: A Design of the Research Project (Pandit, H.N. (Ed), 1969, *Op. cit.*, pp. 3-13.

Panigrahi, D., 'Human Resource Development in Business Administration', B.L. Mathur, (Ed), *Op. cit.*

Parkash, Shri., *Educational System of India: An Econometric Study* (Delhi, Concept, 1978).

Parminder Kaur, and Singh, Bhawdeep, 'Human Resource Development in Rural Punjab' In *U.G.C. National Seminar* held at G.K.I.A.S. in Rural Development (Punjabi University Campus), Damdama Sahib, 22-23 Feb., 1991.

Patel, S.J., 'Educational Miracle in The Third World', *Economic and Political Weekly*, Vol. XX, No. 31, August 3, 1985, pp. 1312-17.

Patil, V.T. and Patil, B.C., *Problems in Indian Education* (New Delhi, Oxford & IBH, 1982).

Perlman, R., *The Economics of Education: Conceptual Problems and Policy Issues* (McGraw Hill, 1973).

Pillai, S.S., 'Educational System and Social Structure', *Educational India*, Vol. 9, March, 1973.

Planning Commission., *The Sixth Five Year Plan: 1980-85* (New Delhi, Government of India).

Planning Commission., *The First Five Plan: 1951-56* (Delhi, Government of India).

Psachorapoulōs, G., *Earnings and Education in OECD Countries* (Paris, OECD, 1973).

Psachorapoulís, G., 'Education and Development—A Review', Pigmy *Economic Review*, Monthly Economic Journal of the Syndicate Bank, Oct. 88, Vol. 34, No. 3.

Punit, A.E., *Social System in Rural India* (New Delhi, Sterling, 1978).

Radhakrishnan, S., *The Creative Life.*

Index